Journey

to the

Center of the Self

by

Maxine Gaudio

*"The longest journey is the journey
inward of him who has chosen his
destiny"*

DAG HAMMARSKJÖLD

Journey to the Center of the Self
Copyright © 2008 Maxine Gaudio.

Haji and Babu Press LLC
Greenwich, CT USA

LIBRARY OF CONGRESS
CATALOGING-IN-PUBLICATION DATA

Library of Congress Catalog Card
Number: 2007941516

Journey to the Center of the Self / by
Maxine Gaudio

ISBN: 978-0-97991-303-7

First Edition 2008
10 9 8 7 6 5 4 3 2 1

"*You are the bell within a bell*
That tolls to tell life's essence.
Without a sound over any distance,
Breaks the spell of silence."

Jiri Sipijlo

With love and respect to

BABAJI

my Mahavatar teacher and

My parents

Doris and Robert

Babaji

ACKNOWLEDGMENTS

When you begin a project such as this you wonder how you will begin and where you will end and if you can really say everything you want to say. So it is with acknowledging all the people that ongoing helped to make this book a reality. All the emotional encouragement, the physical assistance of thoughts and grammar, the finding of the proper printer, the choosing of papers, covers, photographs. The finding of your own memories and putting them in tact in a way that will inform but not purposely injure or insult. I am in Iceland this lovely summer and feeling very grateful to Babaji and I am trying to thank everyone that I can, so here goes:

Thank you to <u>Russ Carpentieri</u> for saying that "one page a day is thirty in a month" and knowing I would never stop at one. To <u>Robert SanGiovanni</u> for his role as the male voice in my chapter on the Unavailable Parent, to <u>Marc Fischer</u> for making every attempt possible to help me when he really could only get the idea of resistance. For this reason I asked him to write his version so I could write my version about something I really did not totally understand.

To <u>Lori and Mike Barger</u> for all their exuberance and detail assistance, to <u>LuLu</u>

deKwiatkowski for all her ingenious ideas of expression and great encouragement. To Jane Kramer for her reading, editing and unlimited support. To all the cast of characters that made up my family and gave me the events to write about. To whomever it was who made rasayanas into rayon (probably a spell check error).

Most especially to Mari Cammarano for things too invaluable to mention and too long a list to print here and to Winnie Staniford who has been there for so many miles along the way and so much clapping and cheering in her very sensible way.

Most of all, I suppose, to every person living and dead who has participated in making my life so far a very meaningful and deeply spiritual experience full of all the ingredients that it took me to grow into what I have become and will become.

TRUTH   SIMPLICITY   LOVE

Table of Contents

LET ME OUT!

I was a small child when I first wanted to come out of the closet. You might wonder how a young child would know anything about "coming out of the closet" but it was not as you would think. "Let me out! Let me out!" I would scream. My parents developed the charming habit of putting us in the closet when we were "bad." I felt like I was in prison and screamed as though through every incarnation. My sister, on the other hand, never wanted to come out. She liked playing with the shoes. We were both shaped by our parents' mistakes, but in different ways. And whether you are the screamer or the quiet one, you too have been shaped by your parents' caring errors. Believe me; whatever they did or did not do they did the best they could.

Perhaps you could say that right from the beginning, I knew I wasn't getting the kind of understanding I probably required. When I refused to eat, my parents made a sign that read, 'Don't Feed This Child'. At the age of three, I was not allowed to sit at the dining room table because my manners were not up to family standards. Our housekeeper, and my keeper, of sorts, Frankie, served me at a separate table with separate tableware befitting a three year old. One day I pretended to be a dog, crawled under the table and bit my father on the leg. He put me outside with my dinner in a bowl.

I prayed for a sister or a brother with whom I could share the things of childhood. When I was four-and-a-half years old that prayer was answered in the form of my sister. How could I have suspected that from that day on the new battle cry in our house would be "Set an example for your sister, Maxine." "Clean the bathroom, Maxine" (in spite of the fact that we had live-in help). "Take the slugs out of the pachysandra, Maxine" (yes, we had a gardener). "Bring in some wood for the fire, Maxine" (yes, the handyman was available for those things). "Set a good example for your sister, Maxine!"

I always felt separate from my family. I wanted them to love me and accept me as I was, but somehow I needed to find a way to be myself and love it. I learned how to undo my parents seeming mistakes and so can you. You can be anything, do anything, have anything and I will tell you how by weaving my tale.

I have lived what many people might consider an unconventional life, although to me it felt quite usual. In the 1940's, when I was 7 or 8, I discovered under some who were considered legends. I have flown planes, jumped out of them, worked on the streets trying to save homeless children in Times Square, N.Y., Guatemala, Honduras and Haiti and helped heal people through Reiki treatments, with cancer, depression, self-loathing, anxiety, etc...some from home, others from the other side of the world without ever seeing their faces..... With all this said, I had parents, I had a child and a grandchild, I have had divorces, romances, highs and lows, love and pain, passions and disappointments, fears and anguishes just like everyone else. I am not super-human, I am no wonder woman (although I have always believed I could fly) I have just trained myself through many practices and modalities such as Reiki and energy healing, meditation, breathing, yoga, tai chi, and most important....COMPASSION....to connect to the incredible life force around us that so many of us take for granted or have forgotten somewhere in the storehouse of our subconscious while trying to keep up in this frenetic world we have all been dropped into. My mission is to let you know and to explain how, through sharing my experiences, to tap into your deeper more powerful side by peeling back your protective skin that has built up through the years and blinded you to the potential and power each one of us possesses.

My friend Lulu said I answer the questions of...What is energy? What is Reiki? Where did we come from (the stork maybe???). Why are we here? Why do we hold onto anger, sadness, aggression, fear, self-loathing, hopelessness, despair and depression? How do we let go of this? Why are these patterns in our life that we continuously repeat? Keep reading and you will learn how to become a higher, more powerful spiritual being. If this is our chance in this lifetime, why not learn to TAKE IT? I doubt that you want it to read on your tombstone..."died with potential"... So, you might as well give it your all, because nobody is going to save you except yourself and although some may walk next to the fire path WITH you, they cannot walk it FOR you.

I will show you, if you allow yourself, how through following the stories of my life, you can break the cycle of following the insanity created in your early years and most likely carried until now.

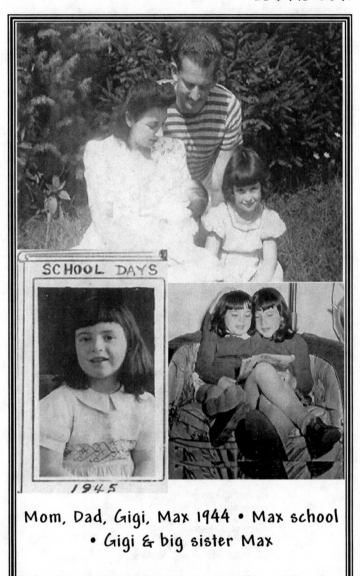

Mom, Dad, Gigi, Max 1944 • Max school
• Gigi & big sister Max

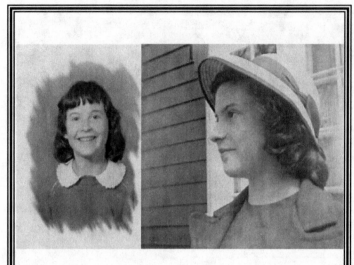

Max, school photo • Max, Easter 1949 or so • Frankie & Max at Gigi's first wedding

Top
Win,
Max,
Lulu

Above
My grandson
Andre, 2007

Max changing Dante (above right),
Dante 1990's

*When his wife asked him to change
clothes to meet the German
ambassador: "If they want to see me,
here I am. If they want to see my
clothes, open my closet and show them
my suits."*

ALBERT EINSTEIN

WHAT'S IN IT FOR ME?

You might want to read this book because it is a book that applies to EVERYONE. If you knew nothing, you would learn from this reading that whatever you have done in your life is OK. It does not really matter if you have had five wives or husbands or many lovers. It matters not about how many different jobs you have had or how insecure or secure you feel. No matter if you have had a life that many consider full of failure, whatever that means, because those people are not in a position to judge anyway, are they? It DOES matter, however, that you find the PATTERN in your life and so this book of mine will, God will' in and the creek don't rise, help you find your pattern started in childhood, start to see what you have learned from the things you have experienced in your life and learn how to use energy work to remove the blocks of the pattern. Find something that you consider divine and surrender to it. THAT'S THAT.

The purpose of this book is to be able to tell people about the story of how I got from point A to point Z. In my case it has been quite a circuitous route, but I digress.

'This is how I became a Reiki Master.' These were the words I jotted down when I began thinking about writing a chapter on surrender.....the most difficult thing I have worked on in my life, I might say, and in retrospect, they are all fairly straightforward, positive and generally feel-good concepts. "Surrender", however, is a tougher nut to crack, and deserves some more scrutiny...which I will do in my chapter on THE EXPERIENCE OF

FLYING WITHOUT A PLANE and particularly since understanding surrender is critical.

I AM SORRY, IN A WAY, TO HAVE TO BE A MITE SERIOUS IN THE NEXT FEW PAGES, BUT I PROMISE A GREAT READ THEREAFTER.

We read books, confide in friends, take classes, experiment with religions, relationships, careers, and invest our hope in therapy. All of us have experienced some form of self-excavation activity, at least at one point in our lives but something still isn't right. Years of scrutiny may have revealed what is holding us back, but we don't break away from its grasp. We may budge from time to time, gaining some leeway but we rebound, settling back into the familiarity of routine. We do not MOVE ON. I discuss a lot of this in my chapter THE DISORIENT EXPRESS.

Those of us who have felt that attention, love, affection, understanding, recognition, are missing from our lives, compensate the void by wearing masks which allow us to negotiate with the outer world on our true self's behalf. The mask we choose is (at once) as liberating as it is confining. We adopt the design that comes easiest for us to wear. It is molded by our life story...in the who, what, when, why, and influences which got us to where we are today. We continue to masquerade because it rationalizes our pain and makes social exchange possible. Too perfect a disguise, however, can lead to dependency and alienation. We become fearful of peeling back the mask. We fear that nothing real is behind it. As a result, we experience misguided answers to life, distorted impressions, empty successes, neuroses, and paralysis. We have confined ourselves with too narrow a SPIRITUAL HORIZON.

Our spiritual horizon is the potential panorama of our being. It is our unbroken view of harmonic strata, which create and manifest topography of psychic energy, particular to our perfect innate state of equilibrium. Introspection can trace our patterns of behavior revealing explanations for what eventually formed our here and now. These patterns are only clues. As such, they point to (but fall short of) exposing how we move on. But they have another purpose. They activate our (unconscious) psychic energy, which is the key to how we emotionally respond to our experiences.

The discovery of who, what, when and why is informative, no doubt about it. It may be therapeutic in that it helps us understand the events of our lives that got us where we are. But how do we get from where we are to where we want/are supposed to be?

THESE ARE, THEN, THE VERY ANSWERS I HAVE LOOKED TO SUPPLY MYSELF WITH AND THEREFORE YOU CAN SUPPLY YOU WITH.

Journey to the Center of the Self

We change our orientation, from the finality of explanations and outcomes to the dynamic/kinesthetic process of creating a path/passage of release by enlisting energy to clear the subconscious/unconscious in a non-invasive way.

It is a progressive, not regressive process that seeks to understand in terms of purpose rather than cause. Our subconscious retains a daily residue of the events we experience, even those we have forgotten (when I learned Tai Chi, the first thing the Tai Chi Master taught was DON'T THINK, use your muscle memory because it is the only way to learn this form). If your muscles can learn and retain, so can you and so do your cells. As a byproduct of our struggle to make sense of our lives we build up emotional plaque. This plaque begins with the original perceived UNAVAILABLE PARENT and takes us on the nightmare joyride of THE DISORIENT EXPRESS.

WHAT'S IN IT FOR ME?

You may have heard about Reiki or energy work, you may have a notion of the divine, and you may even understand the concept of surrender. But you probably do not know about the purification and processing that is a necessary product of this work. This book will help tie in the practice of Reiki to the goals of dumping the old garbage that hampers your life and encourages the breakup of the unwanted patterns that have caused you to act and feel the way you do when you sit alone with nothing to do or think about, nothing to read or listen to, nothing to focus on. The feeling is usually unpleasant, gnawing, sad, raging, remorseful, empty, despairing or just jumpy or anxious. You may have other feelings that are unpleasant enough to make you experience nervousness and the desire to "get going", "get busy", go shopping, go to work, have a drink, have sex, play some kind of sport, work out, go to work or find a project and in general to get away from these feelings.

Each of us seemingly wants to reach the state where we are closer to our higher consciousness, more in touch with our higher selves. There are ways to get closer to or even enter what is called in Quantum Physics, The Unified Field. Very serious sounding but much easier than you may think. They sound like scientific worlds that many of you may never have visited nor would ever be interested in "hanging out" around. I will help you to make it so easy that you cannot help but want to run to get there.

What is purification and how does processing enter into it? Purification is what happens when the energy of the work you are doing hits your cells. The processing begins when the energy reaches the cellular level. The processing begins once the Reiki or energy treatment or even a massage is ended. For young children, who are always open to the energy, this is quite a different experience. This is simply accepted and just IS. By the time you are eight years old the broadcast has static. Up until that time, it is, in most cases, a clear broadcast.

How did this change through the ages? The old paleo-cortex knew how to take care of its body. What it didn't know how to do was have creative thought. And that's what happened when the cerebral cortex was provided. When the larger brain developed, we became thinking creatures. Some might even call it rational. The ability to create with thought, to formulate without the physical reality in front of us, was the job of the cerebral cortex. There are a myriad of other functions of course, but this was a major change from the world of satiating physical needs to producing ideas.

The more we used the cortex, the more we continued to use it. Respect is reserved for science. Higher-order thinking is revered and for good reason. Look at the quality of life changes regarding physical comforts. It started as a physical response and continues as a physical response in many ways. Buildings are not only taller but better and easier to manage. Food is processed quickly and relatively easily. Efficiency and convenience are overwhelming motivators and there is always someone waiting to finance a better mousetrap.

But we have forgotten our old ways. The respect for instinct is gone. Think of an animal that is reared in captivity. The animal will not survive if returned to the wild. Fair enough. But what is it that is lost? It is not the instinct....that instinct is preserved. What to do is not the same as instinct. And the what-to-do part is now gone.

Now it is possible, in this day and age, to also discuss emotions. No one wanted to hear about your emotions when I was growing up (back in the Stone Age). Then along came all of the touchy feely movements of the sixties and "I hear you" took the place of "so what". Having emotions and confessing them was legitimized. Therapists grew in stature and most definitely in income level as people sought out an outlet for something that was just not right. This is a terrific phenomenon...the part where you recognize that something is JUST NOT RIGHT. The solution, however, may not be limited to a situation in which the goal is to apply the cerebral cortex, albeit with the assistance of another, to "analyze". Analyzing does not root out the problem; analyzing labels and identifies and probably even minimizes some of the impact. "Ah, yes" you may say, "that's my mother issue kicking up again". And then what?

Recently Gary Zukav and others talked about the senses. And who understands more than what can be learned from the five senses? Every American youngster learns PHETEC in Science class....the application of the senses to the scientific method. Test, prove, re-test, validate and then get someone else to do the same thing. This is good science. Absolutely. This is how the world factors "senses" into the equation.

Have you ever thought which of your senses is the one responsible for knowing that you have just walked into a room in which there has been an argument? Which of your five senses has told you that? Which of your five senses is responsible when you meet someone for the first time and all the elements are in place...the dress is the style you prefer, the speech pattern is the one that appeals, the hair and face, height and weight, all fall into your preferred categories...but YOU STILL DON'T LIKE THEM? Is this because of any of your five senses? I SAY NO AND SO WILL YOU WHEN YOU FINISH THIS BOOK OF MINE.

"Spirituality is a domain of awareness"
DEEPAK CHOPRA

A RICH BEGINNING

They tell me that on the day I was born my father stood looking at me through the glass in the hospital. I looked right back at him and raised my left eyebrow, as if to say, "I'm here. What do we do now?" It was October 1939, and I was, indeed here.

"Here" meant that I was the first child of Robert and Doris Goodman, of Stamford, CT.

It was the first day of a childhood full of engagement with a loving brilliant, stubborn, ill-tempered father and a mother who was loving, clever, smart but judgmental and overly concerned with other people's opinions. In today's world my mother would have been a CFO of some big corporation (although she always says that if she has to come back to this earth she would like to come back as a rich southern woman).

My father was an aeronautical engineer in the 1930's and 1940's, when the world was just waking up to the idea of technology, and engineers were usually thought of as running trains. He both taught and studied at MIT. He was the product of a fantastic marriage, for his father (a Hungarian Jew born in Budapest) had the audacity to marry my grandmother, a German Catholic. Not really "done" in those days. My grandfather Josef Goodman was a brilliant and entrepreneurial man...a man in many ways before his time. He had become a pharmacist at 16, as well as an herbalist, and by middle-age, had not only bought the pharmacy and the building that housed it (on York Avenue in New York), but had purchased other property in New York and later Connecticut, some rented on 99 year leases. He had married Elsa Stratmann, whose brother, Maximillian was the man I was named after. They lived on Long Island for some time with a summer home in Connecticut and eventually they moved permanently to Connecticut. Together, they decided fairly early on to relinquish the faiths they had brought to the marriage, and become Unitarians at the time that the famous Dr. Holmes was head of the church in New York. He became their minister and friend. They did this, in part, to help their son (my dad) attend a fine preparatory school, and get a leg-up on what would become an extraordinary career. "Leg-up" is a ridiculous pun in this context, but I use it nonetheless. You see, although he had been blessed with a fabulous intellect (among many other gifts); he was also the victim of infantile paralysis, as it was known in those days, Polio in today's parlance. As a result, he walked with a limp for the rest of his days. Debilitating? Sure...to a degree. But I imagine it probably made him even more determined to succeed on his own terms.

In any event, to compensate for the deficiency in his legs, his arms and torso were incredibly developed. My dad was a rock. He rode horses, played the piano and organ, played water polo and wrestled in college. He loved the opera and classical music, as did my mother with whom he most often played duets.

My mother, Doris, was the product of the marriage of Josef (a lot of Josef's, no?) Altstadter. Josef was a mathematics professor from Vienna, Austria who came to the U.S. and quickly realized there was little money in teaching mathematics...so he became a restaurateur. My mother, very bright in her own right, was the comptroller of a department store before the age of 21. She had blue- black hair, green eyes, and pale skin and was very beautiful. Not without her own courage, she flew in one of the first open cockpit planes and danced barefoot in the style of Isadora Duncan.....all very "not of her time". She always liked to tell the story of how she hated to eat breakfast and so her father fed her rich French cheese and caviar to get her going. I remember her mother, my Nana and my great grandmother who came from Romania but had married a prosperous Russian and came to this country with seven fur coats and a heck of a lot of jewelry...so the story goes. I remember her very well because she could never get over the fact that the servants did not kiss her hand. We were, at one time, actually four generations of women.

I remember well my mother reading me mythology and classic children's literature, and I developed a rich fantasy life. I WOULD NEED IT FOR SURE.

The beginning is important. I grew up in a family where my parents were very romantic and loving with each other. They went everywhere together and I never heard an argument. Who knew in the 1940's and 1950's relationships could be dysfunctional and that there was a thing called co-dependency. NOT ME FOR SURE.

The image of love that I was brought up with, the one that my parents outwardly presented looked exactly like what I saw in movies and later read in books. Did I know that it was an ideal that we were all yearning for? No. I thought it was the way it was. On some level, I think all of us want a home that is happy, productive, respectful and loving; where intimacy exists on all levels. Is that what I searched for? Yes. Is that what I found? NO!

A FEW WORDS ON MY CHILDHOOD AND ONLY A FEW.

A great genetic goulash was my family. Into the pot, as I have said, went Russian, Romanian, German/Prussian and Austrian. There were merchants, intellects, artists, and restaurateurs. The ethos of that time in history was change and for some it also included enlightenment and tolerance. Looking at other families (with the gift of hindsight), I suppose mine was special. Special in that I was never truly indoctrinated or grounded in any religious, ethnic, artistic or political doctrine. One of my father's favorite tidbits of wisdom was "pick your friends not by status or background, but by whom you can learn from, and to whom you can teach." It wasn't that tricky a concept to grasp, even for a kid. My family didn't care about where you came from, or what you did; we cared about what someone had to contribute, and whether or not you valued our contribution too.

That's not to say things were all mushy and nice-nice in the Goodman home. Oh no sir. Father was a tough teacher back at MIT before I was born, and he never let that go. He could tell his daughter Max was smart, inquisitive and at times obstinate and contrary....and he liked to keep me on my toes.

"Prove it!" he would say.

"You say you read a book. Well...read another!"

"You read the newspaper. Nice...here's a different one. Read this one too!"

"So...you've formed an opinion. Excellent...Go get someone else's take on the matter!"

He always "encouraged" me to take the other side of an argument so I could understand another point of view and at the same time test the validity of my own argument. I absolutely hated it at the time, but it proved to make a very interesting life for me in which I could perform exceptionally well. By learning to look at all sides I learned to consider my own point of view with confidence.

To offset some of this seriousness, let me tell you that my favorite holiday was Christmas. In fact, my earliest memories are of Christmas. Mother was a perfectionist and so was my father's mother, so the tree had to be perfect. I remember the trees now, and the smell of baking stollen (a sweet Christmas bread made with nuts and fruit) and cookies and so on.

In the beginning, I would write to Santa and get everything I wanted...and more. Then my first cousin, David, came along, and I got half as many gifts as before. Then my sister...fewer. Then a 2nd cousin, Mark, was born, and I got fewer still. I remember saying to myself, "Is that it? Is that how it's going to be from now on? Less?"

I loved Christmas, and believed in Santa until I was at least 10 before the real deal came out. The candy I left for Santa was in my stocking in the morning....this sent me into a real tizzy. Part of this probably had to do with my love of fantasy, stories and myths. My mother would read Greek and Roman mythology to me as bedtime stories and my father would read me comics and we would listen to The Shadow on the radio together.

I grew up looking for the perfect relationship and I wanted what my parents had, even though I hadn't discovered these other ideas yet.

Sure each parent brings strengths and not so strong attributes to the table but they would be known and accepted and worked out. Perhaps one parent can cook better than the other. Does that mean the other just sits and watches football while the cooking is happening? No, not for true happiness to sustain in the relationship. Perhaps one is the breadwinner or makes a hefty sum more than the other. This kind of economic imbalance can be a disastrous recipe in any relationship, leading to bitterness, resentment and insecurity, although it need not be so. We all know now how disastrous it is for women to be put in a prison of servitude to men without intellectual, emotional and financial independence. Balance of power mirrors the natural balance of the universe, yin/yang, light/dark, hot/cold, etc. You cannot sustain one without the other to hold the space. It would be unnatural until we have unity consciousness.

Think for a moment about the expectations of a man going to work for his family, his career desires, hopefully for his self expression in a line of work that is really his bliss (This is, in most cases not the usual, the bliss, that is). He works hard each day. Perhaps he is commuting to another town or city from where he lives. Perhaps it is by train or car and even, in the case of many businessmen, a day or more by plane to do business in another state or country. He puts a great deal of himself into what he is aiming for and now it is the end of the day and he is preparing to return home. He might be expecting that his wife will be at home and he might be visualizing or thinking of how he will be greeted by her and in many cases, his children. He sees her as a place of comfort. He sees her as his reason for all this hard work. He imagines a lovely welcoming, an appreciation for his exertions for her. He is looking for love, appreciation, warmth and a desire from her to "take care of her warrior".

Now, here is the wife, let us say the stay at home wife. She has perhaps after cleaning up the house, making beds, etc., had her tennis game, gone to the gym and had lunch with a friend, if she is lucky this day. Her children are now home from school and she takes them to the food market to shop. The younger child perhaps a little tired is cranky and the older children are bickering amongst themselves, as is often the case with siblings.

They see things on the shelves and want this food or that and her struggle has begun. She travels home and begins to supervise the beginning of homework and the feeding of the younger child. Or perhaps she has had to deliver and pick up one or more of the older children from an after school sports project or instrument training or ballet class. You understand my point. I had a full time housekeeper before parting from my husband and I still had some of these responsibilities. I also was a volunteer and handled all of the finances in the family as well as social planning for my husband and myself. This included a lot of phone calls, etc. I had a gardener and yet I also kept some of the garden for myself.

Although I had a busy day and always made lots of time to be with my son I was quite excited when I knew the time of my husbands return was near. As with most housewives.

I was expecting to enjoy an evening with the man I loved who of course would appreciate the house in order, my looking really good, and a terrific dinner and conversation with him.

Many stay at home wives have the expectations of being appreciated for their work to support the husband in his work.

Now the dance begins. He enters the house with the chaos of the family, children running around and making noise. His wife is exhausted as is he. Each has had their expectations and they were not exactly like the picture now in front of them. "What's for dinner?" he says. "Listen to what happened with the kids today," she says. Already they are on different paths and each most probably feeling unappreciated and disappointed. You take it from here. Expectations are not a good beginning. What might be a better solution would be that before leaving the office or soon after returning home, the husband allows himself some sort of meditation or relaxation technique. At home the wife has done the same. Already the situation will be VERY different. Now, how about a discussion during the engagement process about what each person wants and needs. As an example, both partners might make a list of what they expect and what they are willing to give for those things. Each reads the list of the other and they see if they can agree. Love is lovely, but without these things being discussed before marriage, the love that was promised to last forever...well, let us just say that sometimes forever comes very quickly.

What will we do when we have children? Will both parents work? What will they do to maintain their relationship with each other and still be responsible for the family members? What is each of their views on discipline and schooling of children? What will they do in events of disagreement? Marriage is, as I see it, a contract (my mother tried to teach me that and at the time I thought it was absolutely awful. What about romance?) that should be well planned if people are to go through the lessons of relationship and come out in tact.

My parents decided before marriage that they would always find a way to work things out and make the marriage work for the duration of their life together. To my young eyes and in a time quite different from today, I thought they were "in love" forever. Did I think that my father wanting to do absolutely everything with my mother was really co-dependency? I most certainly did not. I never saw them argue or go out without each other to a movie or a party. There were no nights out with "the boys" or with "my women friends". I never knew that my mother really needed much more space and time to herself than she had and I never realized that my father only wanted to be with her all the time. His best and probably only friend was my mother. He loved to play golf with her and travel with her and do just about everything with her. He truly disliked her not to be in bed with him when he was ready to go to bed and read. This was true even when I was older and visiting and my mother wanted to talk to me a while in the evening. "Come to bed, honey." he would say. But I digress. My point is that we have to have certain understandings of each other before we enter into this kind of a partnership.

You can see how I saw "couple life" as something really easy and great. What a surprise I had in store.

I am most happy now that I look back with different eyes. My dad with all his "prove it" stuff taught me how to reason and lead and not just accept. He made me read many books on a subject and many papers so I would have a look at both sides. This looking at both sides was important in my future. He always told me to take the opposite side of an argument so I could see if I really believed what I thought or was there another way to see the same subject.

As to religion and my father had studied religion and philosophy as a minor at school, his words to me were "The divine should be in you...every day of your life, not just on certain occasions." That was my dad.

At 13 as I discuss in a later chapter, I came across and read what would become my bible. Kahlil Gibran's "The Prophet". All through the many stages of my life, and as I've moved from place to place, Gibran has been ahead of me, already there, leading the way, giving me strength, courage, peace and sometimes solace. What more can anyone ask of a holy book?

So to sum up:

My father taught me compassion.

My mother taught me rules of polite society.

My family taught me tolerance.

Gibran taught me introspection.

I brought irrepressible inquisitiveness to the mix.

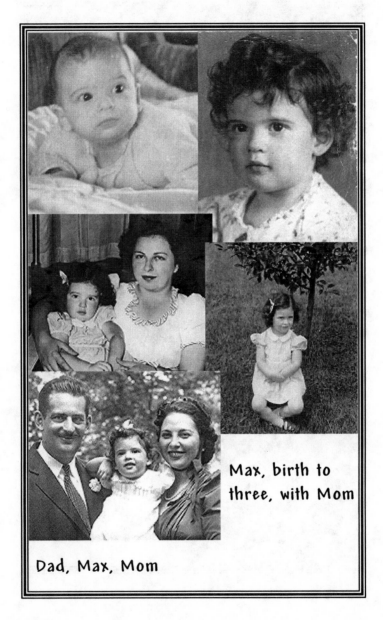

Max, birth to three, with Mom

Dad, Max, Mom

Max & cousin David,
Great Uncle Max,
Mother's parents,

Father's Father,
Father, Father,
Father's parents

Cherry Lawn School graduation with paternal grandparents (above), and everyday lunch at my father's parents' home (below)

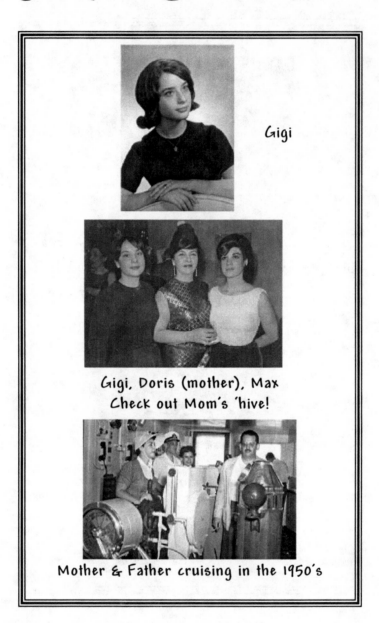

Gigi

Gigi, Doris (mother), Max
Check out Mom's 'hive!

Mother & Father cruising in the 1950's

Nantucket
Surfcasting 1960's

Max and Dad, George & Max's sister Gigi,
Dante and Max, early 1970's

Max's Aunt Helen's 80th birthday with her family

Three pictures of Max
before marriage
early 1960's

Max with cigar on
friend Pete's boat ->

"If the rich could hire people to die for them, the poor could make a wonderful living"

YIDDISH PROVERB

*"Common sense is a collection of
prejudices acquired by age eighteen"*
ALBERT EINSTEIN

THINK ABOUT THESE THINGS. I EVENTUALLY DID, ON MY JOURNEY IN SEARCH OF THE MIRACULOUS.

Old as I am in age, I have no feeling that I ceased to grow inwardly or that my growth will stop at the dissolution of the flesh. What I am concerned with is my readiness to obey the call of Truth, my god, from moment to moment, no matter how inconsistent it may appear. My commitment is to Truth, not consistency.   GANDHI

We do not see things as they are. We see them as we are.   THE TALMUD

In Thy light shall we see the light.   PSALMS 36:9

Om Namaha Shivya (the will of the Divine be done).   BABAJI

Do not follow the ideas of others but learn to listen to the voice within yourself.   Your body and mind will become clear and you will realize the unity of all things.

ZEN MASTER DOGEN

Knowing   others   is wisdom; knowing the self is enlightenment.

TAO TE CHING

Compassion refers to the arising in the heart of the desire to relieve the suffering of all beings.   RAM DASS

IN SEARCH OF THE MIRACULOUS

Sometime in the late sixties or very early seventies, although I still had a "prove it" mind and personality, I saw a course offered called Silva Mind Control. My friend and I went to the initial lecture and I came away thinking "what a bunch of El Toro pooh pooh!" The element that did interest me, though, was the part about controlling your emotions and projecting your mind. The rest, healing, ESP and distance "seeing" were of little believability to me.

Being the kind of person that I was not wanting to judge without trying, I enrolled with my friend for only one of the four twelve hour workshops. We went and for the first day I found it nothing much more than a repeat of the initial lecture. We decided to continue on with the second day and so on it went until we had taken the entire course. One of the first to be given in the early years with many to follow (I think it may still be offered today), I was, as usual, a pioneer in the unbelievable.

With me in this course were three Pan Am Airline pilots and several engineers, psychologists, one scientist of some sort, et al. In all there were thirty of us and of all of us I was the only one not having the experiences that they all were. "What gives?" thought I. On the second to last day they brought in some past graduates of this course to show what they could do...I of course was still finding it all a lot of hooey...BUT, as was somehow always my luck, a very bright young guy kept staring at me and finally we spoke. He was in computer programming, quite new at that time, and he started to flirt while explaining with some degree of scientific knowledge that this was "for real".

He became my kind of Silva Mind Control mentor with an outstanding outcome.

My husband at the time called it my "psychic BS" and was not at all interested. My housekeeper, Jemma, was quite interested, however, and sometime later, together we toilet trained my young son while he slept.

My young friend, Robert Thorne (I guess he was actually a few years older than I, so I don't know why I keep calling him my young friend) called many times each day after that and I brought another guy from this course so we could practice together. I was still convinced that I was not capable of doing this while it was obvious to me that Robert was quite an expert.

As you would expect, I began what would become a long search through books and travel to prove this whole concept to be a fraud......was I ever surprised. The bigger they are the harder they fall, right? Well, I became a believer because I saw what I could do and ONLY because I could have the experience myself. I found that I was not like the others because I was a clair-sensor (only later to become a clairvoyant)... in other words I did not necessarily see things but instead felt them. After some years of using this technique and making my own modifications, I became more than proficient. I was asked and finding people for others, identifying situations unknown to me or the people asking, giving advice (which one of my business clients had been asking for over eight years) and over time being given proof by the inquirer that I was at very least, 85 to 90% accurate. **THE IMPORTANT**

FACTOR WAS THAT I HAD COMPLETE CONFIDENCE IN WHAT CAME TO ME. What came was now presenting itself in a combination of pictures, words, feelings and so on until I realized that mostly, **IT WAS JUST COMING OUT OF MY MOUTH FROM SOMEWHERE.....I WAS NEVER CONSCIOUSLY THINKING OR ASKING FOR ANSWERS.**

Let me ask you this...if you and others were riding in a train, each looking out different windows and I illegally, of course, were riding on the top of the train, which person would be seeing the present? The answer, it would seem would be that all are and that the differences in views of it are imposed only by the limitations of their viewpoint. I, riding on the roof am not looking into the future, but just have a better view of the present and I am using it in a sense system more fully.

I think it may have been Rudolf Steiner who spoke of Spiritual Science as

entering the spiritual world in a way that
makes it possible to distinguish concrete
individual beings and events there.
Through such spiritual research, we
confront the spiritual world in the same
way that we human beings in the
physical world research the mineral,
plant and animal kingdoms. In a large
way this is what Silva Mind Control
teaches. The fact that we can reach into
this world (and the techniques are
taught) to see things in other kingdoms is
the prime experience of this course. It
then adds the "psychic" component. This
idea of an etheric body, an astral body as
well has the corporal body were also part
of the Steiner teachings, which
continued, into his Waldorf Schools for
children. Rudolf Steiner, saw love as a
force in the world.

Steiner was a gifted, clairvoyant
and the founder of **Anthroposophy**.
Completely at home in spiritual worlds,
he oriented his full efforts toward
indicating how spiritual practice can

bring about a truly spiritual culture. Central to his vision was the premise that the evolution of the earth is actually a spiritual one. Steiner believed that prior to recorded history, human beings had a natural, though dreamlike, spiritual perception of the world. Then, for a long period of time, this capacity diminished, as human beings discovered their full individuality and freedom. Further evolution depends upon developing, out of this freedom, the capacity to again perceive the world as the manifestation of spiritual worlds, now in full consciousness.

Rudolph Steiner (1861-1925) was born in Austria and held degrees in mathematics, physics and chemistry at the technical university in Vienna. In 1894 he wrote a philosophical thesis to earn his PhD. This thesis was transformed into a book The Philosophy of Freedom, one of Steiner's seminal works. Next he was selected to edit Goethe's scientific writings at Weimar.

Journey to the Center of the Self

Later he began to speak about his spiritual experiences and described how he was able to make use of his scientific training in such a way that his spiritual investigations could become a science in their own right. During the course of his life he wrote many books, gave over 6,000 lectures (many transcribed into books) and made significant contributions to medicine, education (both Waldorf and curative), agriculture (Biodynamics), drama, dance (eurythmy), sculpture, architecture, religion (the Christian community), and philosophy (spiritual science).

What is Anthroposophy?

Steiner called the results of this spiritual science Anthroposophy (from the Greek meaning the wisdom of mankind) and he founded an international college called The Goetheanum in Switzerland, in 1913. Anthroposophy is a human oriented spiritual philosophy that reflects and speaks to the basic deep questions of humanity, to our basic artistic needs, to the need to relate to the world out of a scientific attitude of mind, and to the need to develop a relation to the world in complete freedom. One's life is based completely on individual judgments and decisions. Spiritual science is a moral, meditative and practical path that cherishes and respects the freedom of each individual. It recognizes that real freedom is actually an inner capacity that can only be obtained by degrees according to the moral and inner development of the individual. The striving for this capacity and the corresponding spiritual development can be greatly assisted through a scientific study of the spiritual nature of humanity and the universe.

I speak more deeply, now, about Steiner and Anthroposophy, because it seems to me that if I had attended one of his Waldorf Schools I would not have had to make such a long and extensive journey to get to where I have come.

Journey to the Center of the Self

It was Joseph Chilton Pearce, author of Magical Child and The Crack in the Cosmic Egg, who said "Ideal for the child and society in the best of time, Rudolf Steiner's (founder of the Waldorf education) brilliant process of education is critically needed and profoundly relevant now at this time of childhood crisis and educational breakdown."

I was still searching. Reading, always a passion, became an obsession. Although this process had begun at around age 13 with Freud, Adler and Jung followed by Gibran, Kipling, Ezra Pound and others, this was a mission in search for the TRUTH. Within a few years I took a book from the library on Yoga. Why? I have no idea. I just wanted to study this thing called Yoga and in those days there were no Yoga Zone or any formal classes available to me. To my family's disbelief, dismay and probably embarrassment, I taught myself Hatha Yoga.

I read the research, stories and case studies of Edgar Cayce, the philosophies of Rudolf Steiner, Madame Blavatski, Krishnamurti and the most wild of all, Immanuel Velikovsky, the concepts of past life regression, the ideas of Gurdjieff-Ouspensky, Dr. Robert S. de Ropp in The Master Game, Psycho-cybernetics by Dr Maxwell Maltz, Body Time by Gay Gaer Luce, Cows, Pigs, Wars and Witches by the anthropologist Marvin Harris on the riddles of culture, The Naked Ape by Desmond Morris and later a book called Super Nature by a student of Morris, Lyall Watson, Psychic Discoveries Behind The Iron Curtain (you can see how long ago that was). I read all the psychological explanations on these matters, I read about Zen and Buddhism, Hinduism and for short periods of time practiced them. I read the Bible, the Koran, the Torah, the Vedanta and so much more...even in the past few years I returned to study Sanskrit recitation from one of the six world famous Sanskrit scholars and Vedic Literature

and Human Physiology by Professor
Tony Nader, M.D.,PhD. In other words I
was on a major hunting trip for
knowledge which has never seemed to
end.

Ultimately, I believed that an
altering in consciousness without drugs
or other assistance was possible.
Remember, this was the time of Leary
and LSD, Richard Alpert later known as
Baba Ram Dass, known for his first book
BE HERE NOW, the Hippie days. Because
information on how to meditate was not
available even in my Yoga books I was
trying very hard to understand how to
reach this level of consciousness. Some
many years later, when I was in my late
twenties, I found a formal Yoga teacher
(Marilyn Roberts) in Greenwich,
Connecticut. and began to learn more
about breathing and other related
information, including meditation. The
teacher was excellent but could, like
others, not explain what to do other than
to "sit". As you have come to know me
you will understand that I made my own

form of meditation and practiced it twice a day after my daily Yoga. My teacher used to go to an ashram (a Hindu monastery) where she had a Guru (teacher). I, not being a very good follower, felt that he did not follow what he preached and seemed to like the ladies a little too much for my taste. I suppose to be completely honest, I went with my now friend, the Yoga teacher, to try and convince her that this was not entirely what it seemed. This was to little avail and so I made a meditation room in my house. After all it had fourteen rooms and was an excellent place to make such a thing for myself. I cannot resist saying, at this time, that when I first visited the home of this Yoga teacher, her watch stopped completely and when her friend came over to visit her watch stopped as well. I was more than confused, but DEFINITELY intrigued. We continue to be friends today.

By now I was teaching my own form of a variety of things and I wanted very much to give some kind of lecture...what a joke. What did I know? I was quite young and had little knowledge as to how to market my ideas. I waywardly obtained a list of names from the local Woman's Club (not the ideal group one might say, but what did I know?) made a poster of a person with the head opening and a person coming out as though breaking out of a shell. I sent announcements and told everyone I knew. They all thought I was "crazy" anyway so this was certainly nothing new. On the fateful night of the lecture I stood up to speak about how we could control our bodies with our minds. Well, if the group had tomatoes in their possession I am sure they would have bombarded me with them. NO the evening was not a success and I went home crying in disbelief. I had the answers. I was sure. I was confident in my speaking and backup research so what could be wrong? Did I ever think that people were in general not ready for such ideas? No is the emphatic answer to that one.

My husband, who was not at all, as a matter of fact, anywhere near, my path and way of thinking was actually quite supportive. He said not to give it up just keep working and believing and see where things went. Fortunately, I took his advice.

Looking back to where I came from, where I have traveled and where I have come is now not only hysterically funny but also quite fantastic. **WHAT THE MIND CONCEIVES AND BELIEVES IT ACHIEVES.** Although I was trained as a musician and scientist I have somehow always taken a chance to ride the pony and see where it would take me. I recommend this to **EVERYONE.** If you don't try how will you know? This is why my then writing helper, Marc had to help me with the resistance part of the chapter on **RESISTANCE.** I understand it in theory but never in practice.

Journey to the Center of the Self

As I describe in another chapter, my life took many turns. I had many jobs and many, many relationships, each one, of course, THE one. But all the while, searching for the miraculous. Many people told me that they could manifest things by just wanting them and focusing their emotions on them always followed by "YOU HAVE TO SURRENDER TO THE WILL OF THE DIVINE!" I understood what "thy will not mine" meant, but I could not even come close to having FAITH in anything but myself. After all, my childhood was not exactly full of situations that created trust, was it?

I went to see the great Sufi leader Pir Vilayat at Columbia University. I was on the same speaking schedule at New York University with the woman who channeled A COURSE IN MIRACLES, and so the beat went on. I was not necessarily less of a scientist but I had definitely greatly enlarged myself spiritually. I was still reading and taking courses and traveling to meet what were considered the spiritual leaders of my day but I was somehow still unsatisfied deep inside.

In the early seventies I had an unusual experience.....REALLY unusual. I had not long finished Silva Mind Control and gone onto past life regressions, etc. but I had now met an astrologer. This was not one of those things I could wrap my mind around either, but when I met Terry Baker she was amazingly accurate. She asked only for my day, month, year and time of birth and also the location of my birth. What could this have to do with my life? How could these planets have any influence on a person's life? WELL, I met her and she was accurate beyond belief. She gave me a 12-month progression of what would likely happen and I watched it like a hawk circling its prey. Every month she was right on. How could this be? It was the future.

Soon after this I had a chart done for my three year old son and my husband. All with the same precise results. I found books on the subject by many authors including a Frenchman named Gauquelin (some of his work was on the connection between planets and professions; even this idea now begins to have a certain scientific respectability). This was, after all, considered a science since the early Chaldeons. Later when I began to read and study the Hindu Veda I found eastern astrology called Jyotish. This method, probably as old as 6,000 years was not based on possibilities and the need for a good psychic, but on rule, laws, and so many things. If one had a great Jyotish astrologer one could know almost anything. It was this knowledge on which Eastern arranged marriages were based....in the event that you might find that interesting.

In 1951 John Nelson was engaged by RCA in the United States to study factors that affect radio reception. By this time it was well known that sunspots are the major cause of interference, but RCA wanted to be able to predict disturbances in the atmosphere more accurately. Nelson studied records for poor reception dating back to 1932 and found, as expected, that they were closely linked to the occurrence of sunspots, but he also discovered something else. Sunspots, and therefore radio disturbances, both occurred when two or more planets were in line, at right angles, or arranged at 180 degrees to the sun. In a later study he refined his method to include data from all the planets and improved his accuracy of prediction to an impressive 93 percent. RCA was delighted, and so, of course, were the astrologists, because this was the first piece of hard scientific fact to show that we could be influenced in any way by the planets. If the planets can affect the sun, then it seems reasonable to assume that they also affect the earth.

I began to study a bit with Terry and talking to her each day really began to make me quite knowledgeable. I continued reading and attending workshops and working as a full time Mother. I was always trying to share my information on a very child-like level so my son Dante could begin to get some early information and techniques. Hard to believe, but when he first cut himself outside with his father, I asked him to use his "white light" (a concept I had taught him) to stop his bleeding....he did within a few moments. All this was happening and I believed it because I could, in some way put a scientific explanation to all of it. Even controlling the sympathetic nervous system was eventually proven at the Menninger Foundation by Swami Ram who spent a week curled in a small box. His blood pressure was lowered, his heart rate slowed, his respiration was slowed to no more than one breath each minute, he reduced his body temperature to what would be considered a lethal level etc. and after a week he left the box, in tact. This gave me a great deal of hope that what I had come to see for myself, although totally criticized by nearly everyone I knew, was now being experimented with...not believed by many...but proven.

Now here comes the extraordinary part. The REALLY extraordinary part for me. I was visiting with my friend Terry, as was our weekly custom. I would have dinner with her and we would do psychic readings for each other. At the end of this one evening, as I was preparing to leave I suddenly saw a man on the wall....not literally, but in my mind. I was not one to have these kinds of experiences unless I looked for some information specifically. No oncoming train wrecks for me, oh no, but what was this? I told Terry that I saw a man, described him and said that I saw him at JFK airport with a briefcase and a white car, which did not fit into the picture. We understood nothing but I knew I would meet him in a few weeks or so. How did I know? I have no idea, I just did and I accepted that.

In about three weeks my son's Montessori teacher, Ms. Trehan, called and asked me if I wanted to join her in the Hindu Temple in New York to attend a lecture by a visiting Swami by the name of Chinmayananda. Well, you can be sure I jumped at the chance. There I sat in a sea of brown faces, crying children and a wonderful cacophony of spicy smells. I did not see the man. Later, after the wonderful talk we went downstairs for an Indian supper. I said to Aruna Trehan that we had to sit at a particular table where I saw THE briefcase. She objected because she saw that two places were taken. None-the-less I insisted and we put our things down and went to the buffet line. Upon returning there were, indeed, two men sitting and eating...one of them was the man from the wall. Do you think he was interested in talking...of course not and I was not as bold as I have become. I had, however, to find the mystery answer here. Slowly we started a conversation and he said he was a professor at NY University Rusk Institute. He was not completely interested in talking to a stranger but rather interested in his friend who was a medical doctor at the same hospital. I asked what color his car was...white...and what he actually did....teach quadriplegics and hemiplegics how to drive. He was leaving on his bi-annual trip, this year to climb in the Himalayas and he was leaving in two days. I asked hesitantly if we could possibly talk alone outside. He was definitely reticent and I was definitely determined. As we walked I asked him what he had been doing three Saturdays previous. If it had been light outside I am sure he would have turned visibly white. WHY? He wanted frantically to know why. I pushed and he said that he had spent much of the day on his knees praying for help. For God to send someone to help him. He said it was the most horrible day he had spent since he skied out of Prague to escape the communists (later to become part of the Olympic luge team). I told him that as weird as it was, I had seen him on a wall and knew he would be here tonight.

This was the beginning of a long and loving friendship with Jiri Sipijlo. It was also the beginning of the idea that it was like being called 007 to see if you wanted to accept the job. How else can I explain it? It was not the last of such occurrences. Many, many people came, each in their own way, for help through me. I must stress that it was THROUGH me, not really me. I was apparently an appropriate recipient of some Divine request sent to me by the most unusual means. ALWAYS UNUSUAL. Most of the time I forget what service I am in but when I remember this story it reminds me with a huge jolt of reality.

Was it a coincidence (unlikely) that when my father died in 1988 I was working for The Streetwork Project, an affiliate arm of Victims Services. I was talking on the street outside the center to a pregnant homeless girl with whom I had a really great rapport. The phone call came and my sister told me to take the next plane home, which at the time was Winston-Salem, North Carolina. It was sudden and unexpected and a great anxious shock came over me. Just that afternoon, at the time my family later told me that he had died, I was overlooking the Victim Services thrift shop. I saw a strange necklace with pieces of turquoise glass ....seven pieces in all with the seventh piece broken. It contained the word of "Allah" in Farsi (the Persian language) and I was incredibly attracted to it....I HAD to have it. My father was, in numerology, a number seven, but this did not register with me until my sister's call.

I usually walked to Grand Central Station for the exercise and to kind of cool down after the night. It was early but my feelings were only a desire for someone to be there who would just hug me for a moment and tell me everything would be OK. So I called my cousin and a close friend but no one was available.

The shock was indescribable. The kids understood better than any adult. I made the decision to take a taxi to get the train as fast as possible. As it turned out I entered the station from an entrance that I rarely entered through. I was coming to the information round in the middle of the station and whom did I see? None other than JIRI. He lived in the city and was waiting for someone to arrive on a train that was late....unbelievable....I had not seen him in many years, but there he was to hug me and let me cry for a moment when I told him about my father. He should not have been there, but he was.

A few months later when I was walking aimlessly down First Avenue asking my father to give me some sign, any sign, that I was on the right path in what I had decided to do, I was almost crying and I looked up and saw, once again, JIRI. He had no business there. He did not even live nearby, but there he was walking towards me. I came to believe that at this time in my life he was my sign.

I would like to think that many people have some sort of experiences like this. Perhaps in dreams, feelings, thoughts, you know, like when you think of someone and the phone rings with them on the other end or a letter from them comes. Sometimes, as it happened with me, someone just appears at that moment of thought. Sometimes we just know, right? It is most probably not something most talk about to each other but I suppose many have them in their own way. I think some people, for instance, have very definite feelings about business deals or whether they should buy this house or that. Things like this are definitely intuition at work (you might read the recent book, Blink to understand what I want to say).

I went on to meet Isabel Hickey, a great Astrologer whose book I considered the best book on Astrology I had ever read. She lived and worked in

Massachusetts and eventually she asked me to speak for her at Boston University.

I interject now to give a little background as to how this came about and where it led. Back in the days of teaching my little mini mind control courses in my living room, much to my husband's chagrin, my husband came home from work and as he walked through the foyer he saw that in the dim light there were about ten people lying on the floor as I directed their minds to see different things. I hear him whisper under his breath "what kind of mystical BS is my wife doing now?" It makes me laugh today. I continue like this until finally I realized that it was tantamount to living with my brother but not what I felt was a husband, in any way except by law. He was a lot of fun and we got along but he was in no way willing to either accept or join me in my new growth. I suppose I cannot blame him. Different minds, different abilities and desire to search. He particularly liked business and making money (which I must admit

made a lot of what I was doing, possible.)
We were growing apart, if indeed, we had
ever been together.

He was my mother in disguise. But
I had no idea of that concept yet. He
taught me a lot about emotional
non-communication. My interest in new
ideas and yet unknown patterns of
connections was not shared. He thought
I was going completely around the bend.
I am sure my housekeeper Nana Pugh
thought the same. I had taken the top
floor of our quite large house and turned
it into a place of teaching and meditation.
Non-mediators' were definitely not
allowed in my little private part of that
space. We had two bedrooms a living
space and a bathroom on that floor and
one of the bedrooms was solely my place
of single retreat. Poor Nana Pugh had to
leave my afternoon tea outside the
room's door. Quite funny to me now, as
I would take tea from anyone anywhere,
now.

It was in this room that I describe that I came to open up my entire electrical system to students of Yoga known as opening of the Kundalini energy in the spine. Without proper guidance this can be quite dangerous, but I had no idea. I just kept doing my little system of meditation and breathing and after some months along came this VERY intense heat and visions and I was afraid beyond description. Each time thereafter, I would have a somewhat similar series of sensations until I began to feel a very REAL change in my consciousness and way of thinking and viewing things, including what people said and how they behaved with each other.

There was nobody I could really share this with because I knew of no one who had experienced or talked of the same experience without a teacher. Once again, on my own and seeking answers, I read so much more. I was a voracious eater of philosophy, the occult (which only means the "unknown", by the way), seminars and lectures by spiritual leaders and the like. Many of them turned out to be charlatans not much to my surprise. I remind many seekers to be on guard for those who claim their way to be the ONLY way and to research carefully every new experience where possible.

Somewhere during this time period I began to spend a lot of time with my friend from "the wall", Jiri Sipijlo. I had given up my private pilot flying and my car racing mostly out of responsibility to my son and because it took time from him. My husband and I had already tried skydiving with my friend Robert Thorne and given it up quite rapidly, at least I had. I had taken a quick trip to London to visit friends and once when I called home my husband said he had jumped and landed in a tree. That was the last he jumped because I thought that was enough of a sign. Besides, this new inner experience was far more exciting than anything I had ever had with anything else.

Journey to the Center of the Self

Because my husband and I had less and less in common I began to go to concerts and lectures with Jiri. He was definitely interested and interesting. He not only was a searcher of sorts and participated in a quiet type of self-testing and experiencing like climbing in the Himalayas to 18,000 feet without oxygen, visiting as the first visitor to Tibet (in the early 70's) but he was also a poet of great magnitude. He gave his time and money to the poor and the physically handicapped in the same spirit that I later did.

I speak of my relationship with Jiri, now, primarily because it was he who was there to spiritually support me when I took a sabbatical from my marriage to sort things out. It was he who helped me to the idea of studying Electroencephalography (EEG) as one of two yearly students accepted at United Hospital in Port Chester, New York. This was to add science to my already avid interest in Biofeedback. In those days Biofeedback was considered a very new thing. Of course, what would you expect from me? He also led me, along with himself, to try Transcendental Meditation (TM) but I will discuss that later.

From this background I went to work as the head of EEG at St. Barnabas Hospital in the Bronx, N.Y. working with the patients of the then famous neuro-surgeon, Dr. Irving Cooper. He created the idea of putting cerebellar implants into the brains of Cerebral Palsy patients and those with extreme seizure disorders. He also was using Cryosurgery with Parkinson patients before the use of L-Dopa.

Well, I gained a tremendous amount of experience and information from that and dared to ask if I could try research with him using Biofeedback. He agreed and the games began. Around the same time, the sabbatical became more of an unofficial separation, which eventually lasted almost 14 years before I actually began divorce proceedings (a story all of its own).

This caused need for money to support my new apartment, etc. and so I was introduced to a psychiatrist who was interested in buying the new biofeedback machines and putting me into a practice with him. This was also a story unto itself as are most things in my life. We went to Colorado to study with the best researchers of the day with The Sarus Institute in Snowmass, Colorado just above Aspen. Of course they had an "alpha/theta" machine that was suppose to measure these brain waves. I learned a lot, received a certificate but gave them a lot of trouble because I had seen through my EEG experience that particularly the brain wave called theta was only experienced "eyes open" by young children. Adults required being almost on the level of sleep to produce these waves. You will understand this by thinking of how you, from time to time, experience the feeling of seeing pictures while not being entirely asleep nor entirely awake (although, when I began

Yogic Flying I experienced being in Theta and could do it with my eyes open).

Think of it like this: Beta (13-30 Hz or cycles per second) is used by part of the brain during our usual ordinary consciousness during our day. It is used in linear, piece- by- piece thinking. Alpha is for relaxation and these waves (8-13 Hz) begin to occur when you close your eyes and relax deeply. It will also occur in parts of the brain when you open your eyes and then close them. Alpha will "kick in" for a few moments.

Theta waves (4-8 HZ) follow and then delta waves (0.5-3.5HZ) are produced during the deepest recuperative sleep times. (ONE MIGHT ALSO NOTE THAT ZEN MASTERS HAVE BEEN PROVEN TO BE FULLY AWARE AT THIS LEVEL.) Some years ago in a book called Psychic Discoveries Behind the Iron Curtain, experiments were made and it was then proven that psychics operated, consistently, at about 8-10HZ. We generally go through all these brain wave levels during a normal night's sleep but we can train ourselves to use these different levels of consciousness by a variety of methods including, but not exclusively, meditation.

AS YOU MIGHT OR MIGHT NOT SEE, THE TEACHING ON MY LIVING ROOM FLOOR AND THE TECHNIQUES I CREATED WERE ALL TO END IN USE WITH MY BIOFEEDBACK PATIENTS...ALWAYS LOOK FOR THE PATTERN.

I eventually met a great M.D., Jack Tobin, who had some peripheral interest in what I was doing and offered me space in his professional building. I took it. How exciting was it for me to actually be making a living doing what I loved? I hung my professional shingle and began a whole new segment of exploration. A few years later I moved to my own place in the building in which I lived so that I could work and still be home in time for my son when he returned from school.

Coinciding with this event was the appearance of a medical director from GTE who loved what I was doing and eventually, unbelievably, had the courage to mention it at a meeting with other corporate medical directors. This led to a contract with UniRoyal Corporation. This was an experience all to itself. I was in my early thirties and after I "sold" the big executives on what stress did to them, etc., I left thinking "now what will I do?" I have sold it but can I really produce it? I must say I was not always as confident as I later became. Of course I produced an incredibly successful program and this led to more and more corporate work. Please do not think that for one minute my friends or family were proud of my work. Au contraire, my friends, they were only more and more concerned about my terrible future because I had made another ridiculous decision.

From this came local and NY City newspapers writing articles on this "crazy" thing I was doing. Business Week did an article on stress management in corporations and I was one of the people written about (of course when I excitedly called my parents and told them to get the magazine it only took four days for them to run right out and get it and about five minutes to complain that if I had been more available the entire article would have been on me.)

BIG PATTERN HERE, MY DEARS. I THOUGHT ABOUT ALL OF THIS ON A PLANE RIDE TO SEE THEM AND REALIZED THAT I DID NOT NEED ANYONE, NOT EVEN MY PARENTS, TO APPROVE OR GIVE ENCOURAGEMENT. I, LIKE YOURSELVES, KNOW EXACTLY HOW GOOD YOU ARE AND YOU NEED NOT EVER LOOK TO OTHERS TO BE SURE. A TOUGH LESSON, BUT A REAL LIFE CHANGING ONE. TRY IT. SEE WHAT IT DOES FOR YOU.

At the same time my parents were concerned about what I was calling a career. They were calling it folly and telling me to do something more sensible and believable. If you understand that today Biofeedback is now old time stuff that is considered mainstream you will understand why I was always before my time and therefore always in trouble with someone who thought what I was thinking was crazy and what I was doing was an even worse disaster. What do you do for a living would come up at parties and when my answer was that I was a Biofeedback Therapist they went for another drink. I on the other hand was close to stopping the parties all together.

In about 1975 or 1976 my parents, who had already moved to North Carolina, had convinced my sister and brother-in-law with their children, to move there as well to be near them. Soon thereafter they began the "persuading" of the "other" daughter...me. I liked visiting but was not really interested in making the move. My astrologer, Isabel Hickey, told me it would be a terrible place for me and a very disastrous turn of events might happen there. My Mother, on the other hand took the time one day while we were swimming at the club, to mention that she and my Father would not be alive forever and would it not be wonderful for the whole family to be together. That was the manipulative and key sales pitch for me. Not about their longevity, but about the family being together. I always had my illusions about this (not knowing at the time that they were just that, illusions).

Despite all the warnings I received, the fact that we could all be together and my sister said she would open a Biofeedback Clinic with me, overrode them. Her husband would be the Medical Director and we would all open an office together. My brother-in-law already had an enormous job but could do this by taking a small amount of time to see our patients before they saw one of us. My sister was a family therapist and was interested in learning use of the biofeedback machines and my techniques. It seemed a perfect move.

The perfect move turned out less than perfect in the terms in which I was looking at it. It did, indeed, show me so much about life and myself in ways I never expected. I found many people in the little spiritual community to be envious of what I was doing and the popularity of my offerings. Most of all I learned a lot about my relationships with my family, friends and so very much about expectations of them and myself. It helped me, almost more than anything, to understand compassion, rage represented as anxiety, fear represented as anger, that my Father was not the problem that I thought he was and more than ever that I had an enormous amount of courage and will, that when I used it, saved my life or at least my mental life.

My sister and her husband backed out after I had signed a lease in a great building with a lovely office and a great view...bully, bully for me. Again, a huge responsibility but an equally large opportunity.

I moved to a great house, bag and baggage, son and all. On the day I moved in I was surrounded by boxes and boxes, my son asking what we were going to do for fun today and most importantly...my parents were at the club playing golf and my sister was who knows where. Did anyone ask Dante and me to come to dinner? No! This was the beginning of my astrologer's prediction. At the time it was a completely devastating experience. A full feeling of betrayal by my family. Oh, big surprise, right? None of you have ever had an experience that left you feeling like this, right? If not I will just expect it was denial. **ULTIMATELY, IT TURNED OUT TO BE THE JOURNEY THAT REALLY LED ME TO EXPAND MY SPIRITUALITY AND CONSCIOUSNESS. WHEN YOU FEEL AT YOUR DEEPEST DESPAIR...AND I WENT THERE, BELIEVE ME...YOU CAN BEGIN TO**

GIVE UP SOME EGO AND START THE PROCESS OF SURRENDER. LOOK AGAIN FOR THE PATTERN...IN THIS CASE; EXPECTATION AND DISBELIEF IN WHAT I REALLY KNEW INSIDE WOULD BE THE CASE. HOLDING ONTO THE POSSIBILITY OF HAVING MY FAMILY, AS I WANTED IT, NOT AS IT WAS.

During my time in North Carolina I opened the clinic and commuted every two weeks between my clinic in Winston to my clinic in Connecticut. I must admit that there was something freeing in this. I stayed in the apartment of my famous architect friend, Victor Bisharat. A true genius and a true heavy drinker. He was also a philosopher, musician and a great friend. His son, Toby and I became great friends and we all "hung out" together. I stayed in his apartment when he was in the Middle East and had a whole different set of friends there than in Winston. I had a different car and a different boyfriend and a different surrounding in each place. It had its advantages. People loved when I came and when it was becoming average I would return to my other life and everyone was happy to see me there. There was also at that time, a gentleman by the name of Victor Shamama with whom I had been having a very long term love affair. He could never get used to the idea that I had actually moved away from him and although we chose not to see each other very often, he always stayed in touch by phone when coming or going into or out of the country. I saw him about eight years ago when I was teaching in Florida and it was amazing how old he had gotten. Not me, of course, but him. He would never allow me to know his age anyway and I had known him by then for over twenty five years. Well, eventually I closed my business in Connecticut to be with my son and concentrate on my Winston business. Dante, my son, wanted me home even when he was in school so he could feel like I was like other mothers. This is about the time that things began to close in on me. In the south I was "really" different. I drank espresso coffee, ate hummus and couscous and most of all I did not drink or have an addiction to sports. I felt isolated to say the least. This isolation eventually led me to the charming experience of anxiety or panic attacks.

I am reminded of a very funny (but not so funny) story. I was working everyday with my biofeedback patients, now in an office with a psychologist and a psychiatrist and now still having these dreadful anxiety attacks. I used to put the electrodes on my patients, hook them up to the EMG and temperature machines, and begin the process of relaxation and feedback. I remember how funny and yet frightening it was that I might be helping someone with relaxation, etc. while the possibility of my own experience was looming large in the forefront of my mind. What if I passed out while my patient was in the chair, eyes closed, and the time passed and the patient opened his or her eyes to find me in this condition? Or worse yet, the time went too long and they did not know what had happened, leaving them to go on and on without hearing my voice. You see the irony, but there is also pathos here.

This led me to examine, closely, what was going on with me. I felt alone, betrayed by my family, responsible for myself and my child and then one day......a great AH HAH! I was filled with rage that was so suppressed that it seeped out as anxiety. I began to see how my childhood and the players in it had let up to this. That my somewhat tyrannical father was not the whole problem at all. It began to emerge that my mother was, indeed, the perceived unavailable parent.

My practice was good because all the docs would send me their worst patients. They referred those who had headaches or depression or backaches for years. I of course, would change all that through my Biofeedback techniques employing **MY ORIGINAL METHODS OF RELAXATION THAT I HAD DEVELOPED AND USED BACK ON MY LIVING ROOM FLOOR. SEE THE PATTERN?**

In the end I really could not win. The doctors were happy that their patients were cured or at least better but they had not been the ones to do it. A real double bind.

Back on the oasis and it really felt like that to me, I was stuck, relieved only by the friends from Connecticut who would occasionally find there way down for a week or two to visit. I had the opportunity to appear frequently on the local TV station and give lectures at Wake Forest University or the hospital. Not enough to keep me satisfied. I wanted to really be of service but my time had not come. When I was written up in Business Week, I got a call from a hospital in Indiana just outside of Chicago. They wanted me to come and speak to executives about stress. It was winter and I was so anxious myself that I felt like a fraud. I asked for an extraordinary amount of money thinking that they would turn me down. I asked my father about this and he only laughed that anyone would pay to hear me speak about "this nonsense".

They checked out my credentials with all the companies I had worked with including Reynolds Tobacco Health Clinic patients. They called, much to my nervousness and hired me. They were billing me as "Nation's Leading Expert" and it made me a wee bit uncomfortable. I was still in my thirties and I felt a lot of responsibility talking about what I knew was true and proved but what most thought was way off the path. Another test and another fear to overcome. It was the one and only lecture series I ever actually prepared for with written lecture notes, etc. My sister flew out with me and we were stuck in a snowstorm for a while in Kentucky. They sent a special plane so I guess there was no way out of this one. When I look back it gives me a complete belly laugh. Now that nothing much bothers me and not too much can set me off my center it is hard to look back and see how far I have come. I thought at the time that I was pretty far ahead. What a lot of ego that was.

I joined with a professor at Baptist Memorial Hospital and with the hospital's backing, we did workshops on Biofeedback and individual practices for physicians. In other words we were talking things like "Welcome to the Machine" which involved learning the use of Biofeedback equipment and "Physician Heal Thyself" which of course went over like a flatulence in a diving suit. The hospital wanted us to withdraw that title from our agenda and so I learned more and more about the system. These workshops went extremely well and I taught a lot and learned a lot.

Journey to the Center of the Self

I remember very well at one of the last workshops at the Hyatt Hotel, meeting a man that we let take the workshop even though he was not really qualified as a physician or medically trained person. My partner and I just felt somehow that he should be there. I was a cigarette smoker at the time although I never talked about it or let anyone know. It just did not seem to fit with "the program" but I loved those Camel regulars so much. They were there for me when nothing and nobody else was. How I laugh in amazement when I look back on that piece of habit now. But I digress, as usual. This young man kept telling me that if I would go to where he was in North Carolina he would show me what he did with certain sounds on his organ. He told me that I was eating dead food and that my smoking was stopping my progress. He said I was way too advanced not to see what he could see. I, as you know by now, gave him a VERY difficult time. Prove it, I would say. If you can really do these fantastic things you would not need any sounds or props, I would say. All the day I challenged him. I was once again a know it all fool.

On the second day, during a break in the seminar, I challenged him to go to another room with me and in the thirty minutes available to do "his thing". WELL, let me say this about all that. He played some incidental music, sat me on the floor in the crossed leg position, asked me to close my eyes and began to run his hand up and down my spine. It was like some kind of altered state that I entered into, almost immediately, totally beyond words or explanation. I was moving into space. The colors and pictures more colorful than any dream state. I was totally aware. All my chakras (energy centers to be later explained) were coming alive. I felt more love and peace than I could ever imagine. I was euphoric. To this day I have never felt anything to equal this exact experience. It was unimaginable. When I left the room and walked around the hotel with the little time left, I could see the energy of everything. The plants were so alive. I saw the aura (energy field in colors seen around people) of everyone I passed and I immediately knew his or her entire life in a flash. I was completely overwhelmed. I loved and respected everything and everyone I encountered.

I finished the morning session with an entirely knew vision. I laughed and taunted this guy no more, au contraire, I was in complete awe. He was nothing special in his ideas or mindfulness, but he had this rare and unusual power. We adjourned for lunch. I saw all the food on the buffet table. Most of it was totally unpalatable even to look at. DEAD. The food was dead. There were a few exceptions. The vegetables were extremely alive as were the fresh fruits. I could not eat anything that I would have eaten a few hours ago. Now it was clear and so was the ridiculousness of my smoking habit. I was aware that at some level I was trying to kill myself. Oh dear!

I finished the seminar and went home to my parent's house.

Waiting there for me were my family and my son. I had a friend, my old yoga teacher, visiting me and attending the seminar. I was able to see everything about everything all the time. I heard things and saw things I had never seen before. I was afraid I was going mad but it was simultaneously a most exciting experience. My family was their usual annoyed selves. They were disapproving of everything I was doing and I certainly could not share with them the things I was presently experiencing. I saw them so differently. The feeling of love and peace were present even in the middle of this messy family business. The experience lasted, unfortunately, for only about three days but I knew that I could one day find it again. I was a different kind of believer now that I had a new sight and it was totally experiential. No words, just a new form of seeing and hearing and feeling.

You might expect that I would have changed my eating and smoking habits, but no, not yet. That came later. I had been vegetarian for seven years in the late sixties and seventies but it was not until October 6, 1981, (funny how you never forget the date when you stop a big habit) that I stopped smoking and changed my eating habits completely.

But once again I must go back and finish what I was saying. During the same time that I was doing these seminars and seeing private patients, I began writing and recording the very relaxation tape that I had been using with my Biofeedback patients. I would put them in a room without a window, in a recliner chair, cover them with a blanket, hook them up to the equipment and take their history. Somehow, I really cannot explain, ALL of my patients must have really trusted me because I would begin to explain what I thought the pattern was and how the machines worked and then I would begin the relaxation by personally reciting my techniques, which were really like a visualization. They could listen to their response on the Biofeedback machines, etc. By the time the session was over they were very relaxed. This would go on for a few weeks or perhaps a month and headaches would stop, backaches would stop, anxiety would greatly decrease, colitis problems would resolve and mostly all central and sympathetic nervous system symptoms would resolve themselves. Many asked me to tape for them. **IF YOU FOLLOW THIS YOU WILL SEE HOW THIS TIME LED TO RADIO, TV, CORPORATE WORK AND MOST IMPORTANTLY THE TAPES THAT WERE BOUGHT AND SOLD BY DAYTIMERS OVER 30 YEARS AGO. THIS BRINGS US TO A PRESENT REMASTERING OF THE SAME TAPE INTO A CD. DO YOU UNDERSTAND THE PATTERN OF HOW ONE THING INTRODUCES ITSELF INTO**

SOMETHING ELSE AT A DIFFERENT TIME?

Of course when my mom and dad would see me on TV and I would ask what they thought, they would tell me that I talked a lot or I needed a haircut. So much for family support. I suppose that to them, at that time, I was unbelievably off the track. They must have asked themselves what kind of profession was I entering into and how was that ever going to lead to a reasonable and responsible life.

It was now a time to begin the idea of serious change. I was going back to New York City from time to time and the feeling of belonging was much stronger here than where I was living or imprisoned, it seemed. I found a charming apartment in an old Gothic house. It had been the reception and music rooms and had two huge fireplaces. The living room was hand-cut oak paneling and the floors were all inlaid wood in beautiful patterns. The ceilings were twelve feet high. It had two bedrooms, mine being in the turret and semi-round with stained glass windows from floor to ceiling and the other had been the glassed in porch. It was a perfect stage for my next performance.

It was here that I later housed my first Reiki Practitioner and my first Reiki Master from Croatia. But I am getting ahead of myself.

Somewhere during the trip to bring my son to visit his father in Connecticut, I met a very nice man from Persia. He saw me a few times and he went back home and I went on my usual trip back to North Carolina. Soon thereafter, the hostage crisis broke out in Persia (Iran) and my friend barely made it out with his young daughter, Shiva. As you would already presume, I became the one to take care of this adorable little four and a half year old child with dark hair and big soulful black eyes. She had a serious blood disease and she and her father needed me to help them, of course, what else. I put her in school. Within a month or two she was speaking English and correcting her father. By and by I helped him get his green card here; got Shiva the necessary medical care and life went on. Only now she is thirty-four years old and has developed into a young woman of great proficiency whom I feel is my second child. We have such a similar way of thinking and our minds explore in the same direction. It was a great joy recently, to see them once again, her mother and father and to spend time in Washington, D. C. with her. Because of many things, including the amount of time it took to get his family on their feet as well as the fact that I was finished with this portion of my life, I had now decided to make some changes.

I packed up in North Carolina and began living in Connecticut. It was still necessary to commute to my practice in Carolina while working in Connecticut with corporations. It gave me a chance to earn money, do what I wanted by helping people and at the same time gave me a moment to rest and recover myself from the agoraphobia. To live alone with my son and not be afraid to drive or travel alone was not entirely easy, but I was extremely focused on healing. I was too afraid not to. Dependency was not my forte.

It was a difficult time in many ways but then I had been under stress since October 7, 1939 at around 1:53 A.M...the date of my birth. After all, was this not my chosen path? I see it now but then it was just one torture after another. I really needed a paradigm shift, to say the least.

Things in my profession began to slow in the early 80's and I wrote a book and tapes called Creative Union. The creativity and being in a recording studio again was just so fantastic. I never really cared about the money or saleability or my creations, only the process itself. I wrote the script, recorded myself and designed the cover and container. It was about having a great relationship.

This, after all, was something I knew more about than anything else. At the same time I created a golf tape and a progressive relaxation tape. I tried promoting everything. I took Creative Union to the head of Revlon International because his daughters were my friends and they thought he could lay out a marketing plan. This led me to Helen Gurley Brown at Cosmopolitan Magazine. She loved it and gave me many suggestions as to how to promote it. As usual the time was many years too soon. I would say that I was disappointed, but I was not. I enjoyed all of it. I was scared about what to do next, but I was enjoying myself.

As things began to change and I stopped commuting so my son could have more stability, my money became short. I needed a major surgery and I had no health insurance. This led me to a simple job in a travel agency, which made a huge point in my life. I was doing a "menial" job compared to my knowledge and training and yet I had a huge mental opening.

I recognized one of the most important lessons of my life. **I COULD PICK PAPERS IN THE STREET BUT THAT DID NOT MAKE ME A PAPER PICKER. I WAS STILL MYSELF.**

That recognition, coming in a moment, changed so much for me. I realized that you are always who you are NOT what you do. This is why so many men and I suppose women as well, feel that they lose their identity when they lose their job. Not so, but until you understand this idea you can be quite miserable and feel useless and unworthy at a time of a job loss crisis. It is indeed, an opportunity getting ready to happen. Change, although inevitable, is something one needs to look forward to not cower back from. If you assess the things that have come from change, looking back, you will see how much they helped you grow.

So now I knew that I did not need anyone's approval or disapproval of anything I did and also that I was who I was not what I did. What a relief. This has changed the entire course of my life. Making a decision and sticking to it became easy. I was more sure of myself than ever. When you come to this place in your life, you too will be changed forever and only in a most positive way.

Following these times I developed a relationship with a man from Jordan. He was considerably younger than myself, which was unusual in itself as I had always been with older men. Everyone said I was foolish because he would surely leave me eventually. I said that even older men leave women. It was certainly no concern of mine. As the relationship began to fail I began to realize the idea that he was, underneath, so much like my Mother. I knew it would never really work. It lasted for four years and then I finally said that he had to leave. We both cried for a long time and continued to see each other through the grieving period. I had learned the lesson of a lifetime in relation to what I had been doing most of my adult life. It was quite clear that I was looking for my Mother and picking men who fit the bill.

Unfortunately, I was more like my Father and therefore, within my theory yet undeveloped completely, or proved to me for that matter, and if I continued to be attracted to the same type of men my relationships would most certainly be doomed. I could have transcended all of it but I was not that far along yet.

I had developed a lower back problem at around the same time that this relationship was failing. Duh, I cannot imagine why. Feeling unsupported perhaps? After I healed and separated from this gentleman, I looked for a part time job. My back continued to need nurturing and so twenty hours a week was what I decided on. I had many choices, but the one I chose was at Friends of Children. It was a not-for-profit organization that dealt with children in Haiti, Guatemala, Thailand, and Honduras and to a lesser degree, the United States.

Why I introduce this information now may seem out of order but indeed, it is not, for it is here that I began an entirely new profession and path. YOU WILL SEE THE PATTERN FROM EARLY ON TAKE ITS PLACE IN THE OVERALL PICTURE.

Within a short time I was asked to take over as Executive Director. I suggested to the founder that I was not interested and that she might want to consider a sabbatical. I agreed to six months (although it turned into a year) and with that she put everything on my desk and left. She never helped or taught. I was quite unsure of what to do first. I had never been to a Board meeting, never planned a budget, and never sought to solicit funds or in-kind goods from the private sector or from corporations or grants. I found though, that all my life training and my outgoing personality helped me learn quickly. It really does not matter what or how much I did. What does matter is that I found for the first time that WITH THE EXCEPTION OF A FEW THINGS WHICH REQUIRE A LOT OF TRAINING (such as surgery, civil engineering, things of this nature) I COULD MOST PROBABLY DO ANYTHING I PUT MY MIND TO DO. WOW! WHAT AN IDEA, NO?

As I mentioned in the beginning chapters, this led me to many new social service types of work. These endeavors helped me to see that they were removing many of my childhood problems (abandonment issues for one). I then began to piece together the idea that whatever I did was a reflection or opportunity to learn about myself through my reactions and in return the reactions of people to me. I worked, as I have said, in Times Square, N.Y., Haiti, Guatemala and Honduras and eventually was asked to join the Board of Directors of an international advocacy organization for children living in the streets. This was Childhope and was backed by UNICEF and the Carnegie Foundation. This organization was initiated as a movement on behalf of street children. The Board contained some of the great workers in many countries working on behalf of children in this condition. Some were known in worldwide circles and were most sincere in their efforts to make change. I of course was attracted to the possibility of taking action on the rights I so strongly believed in.

By and by I came to see that my forthrightness was by no means appreciated. I was not a natural diplomat and had a tendency to speak the truth as I experienced it...even at meetings at the UN. This naturally got me into more trouble than I wish to remember. I did, however, learn a lot about politics as a whole and most certainly how if I was surrounded by people who wanted to rise to the top, whatever that means, they did not stop at taking my hard work and ideas as there own.

After much work and a somewhat naive idealism, I left this organization behind. It was my idea that a movement on behalf of anything should move, not talk about how it was going to move.

I subsequently joined and worked for a small outreach organization called STREETWORK, which was a part of Victims Services Agency in New York City. There I used my skills of obtaining in-kind goods from companies and eventually doing events to raise money for the kids I worked with on the streets of New York. My idea was to start a small factory that would produce briefcases made of cans that I had seen made by children in Senegal. Victims Services eventually agreed to take me on and try to get grant money to start this venture.

After what seemed to me, an eternity, I realized that my project would never be a priority and I was beginning to once again encounter the ever present politics that is so pervasive in most organizations. This was appalling to me because I was a real cause fighter and I saw things quite simply. Move directly and do what you have in mind. I had slowly developed a group of about 75 young volunteers, many from large Wall Street firms. They helped with all of my fund-raising endeavors and when I decided to start my own organization, Kids with Kids, for 25 unwed mothers with babies living essentially in the street, they rallied behind me.

This all led me to a woman, Lolita Fonegra, who was the Assistant Director of Hispanic Affairs for the Governor's office of the State of New York. We did many things together and she came on my Board of Directors. It was she who called me to ask if I would join her in meeting this fellow who had come from Croatia via Argentina and was living with a Cuban friend of ours. I wanted to refuse, but the circumstances dictated that I not decline. He was supposedly a

Reiki healer and was working in New York for just a few days until he went to Canada.

We drove to the city and met him. What did I see? I saw a tall, rather serious man in a cheap gold rayon kimono with rosary beads and a cross around his neck What, I thought, have I gotten myself into this time? I tell this story as a lead into what followed. He put my friend on a table, put his hands on her eyes and face and began whatever it was he did. As for myself, I could see energy coming in the top of his head and leaving through his hands....so what I thought, the guy is some kind of hose. I was used to seeing the energy and I was still very much an intellectual, altogether, a bad combination for spiritual endeavors. Who knew? Had I learned that I had to LOSE MY MIND AND COME TO MY SENSES? Definitely not.

As I sat looking at the energy move and hoping I would have my turn and we

it to nothing else but the energy through the hands of the Croatian healer.

Ok! I am working at a large agency in New York as the Director of Public Information and Development (you thought perhaps that I was a flaky granola?) all the while continuing to move forward with my own charity, Kids with Kids. Now I have a healer living in my somewhat small apartment. My phone is ringing off the hook with appointments for him. My home is invaded daily and nightly with people. I am cooking and caring for the needs of this guy whilst taking daily treatments. I continue to commute to the city three days a week. Now comes the real fun... he sits me down and says "God loves you, I vill (will with an accent) stay four weeks". Oh my! You see, here I go again? I am fascinated by what I am experiencing...a kind of cellular detoxification. I am also enjoying the meditation circle that we have formed on Sundays as well as having someone to join me in my normal daily meditations.

I learn new chants... I am starting to believe...a little.

I asked some of my professional friends (a few doctors, nurses, therapists, etc.) who had a variety of physical problems (backache, headaches, knee problems and so on) to come and take the challenge with me. I wanted to see if changes would occur both from a subjective AND objective point of view. THEY DID. No question, they did occur and there was no logical explanation. Everyone had symptom relief and very deep relaxation. Everyone had a lasting experience. My dear friend, Dr. John Tobin and a research pediatric doctor, Thorston, from Germany working at the hospital at Valhalla (who, just as a side thought, taught me a lot about an ancient Viking and German divining technique called Throwing The Runes) were amazed to the point that they both took the Reiki course we offered later on in the year. I speak with his teacher from Croatia and jokingly say "when are YOU coming to America?" to which he replies, "never! I never leave my country". Ok, good, one less and I was only joking anyway.

I have many unusual experiences with this guy and the energy, very unusual experiences. Am I interested in learning how to do this? NO!

He spends his month and leaves for home. About three week later I receive a call from him saying that his teacher, Ivan Bakic wants to come and meet me and he will bring him. I, thinking in my now perverted mind that I should take the risk because I feel huge shifts are about to occur in my life, say yes, but only for the month of July. He speaks to Ivan and we all agree. Ivan Bakic calls me, always with the beginning "Ivan Bakic here". His voice is deep and energized. I imagine him with dark hair and blue eyes. I must make many arrangements for him to come...even for a short visit because his country is, at that time, at war. I make the arrangements. The first healer arrives and stays for a week to be sure that all is in order for the great coming.

My friend, the healer and I go to JFK to meet the flight. I am so excited to see the person I have been talking to. People begin to come out of customs. My friend and I are looking for this great looking, magnetic fellow of immense stature...the healer says "there he is"...oh, gosh, this cannot be...a man resembling the singer Tiny Tim is coming towards us with his hair askew, his jacket hanging more to one side than the other, his pants half stuck into his socks...oh, my gosh. We greet and move toward baggage pick-up, etc. We get the car and begin the ride home....in a matter of five or ten moments everything appears different. Bakic is magnetic, fascinating, brilliant and immensely spiritual. How lucky are we? No more judgment, let's just see what most unusual events will transpire...and I know they will.

What a fantastic energy. I cannot even describe what happens or how I feel. My friend experiences the same things, but working in open-heart surgery as a Physician's Assistant, he looks at things with less regard and awe. Who cares, this is really an exciting experience for me. We talk and talk and talk. Bakic says he came mostly because Babaji told him to come and that he really wanted to see the person that could live with such an astrological chart as mine. What? Am I some kind of freak? No, just a person with a difficult chart.

I know that I never prefaced this story with this. Some months before, maybe six or seven, I had been diagnosed with a pseudo-tumor behind my right eye leaving me on medication that did not allow me to see well, feel well, or make it across a room with out losing my breath. I could not work. I stayed home and planned my Kids with Kids project. The IRS wanted to audit me because they did not understand what I did working on the street with kids, I was in Federal Court with a case that my ex-husband was dragging me through and my estranged son was asking me to help him into a recovery program for his alcohol and drug problem. I was going to a New York specialist on a regular basis for his special brand of fear and to have the pressure in my eyes checked. This was all a bit much even for me. I was distraught or perhaps completely beside myself.

One morning, in a really deep moment of despair and hopelessness, not knowing what to do or where to turn, I went into my bathroom to do my morning ablutions. Suddenly, between my sobs, I, like some crazed woman, began to talk to my dead father. "I surrender," I said. "Please, I never listened to you before and you never exactly guided me, but now would be the time." definitely, now WOULD be the time. I did not want to follow anymore frivolous paths or ideas. I needed help.

"Please put me on the path you want. I mean it, I surrender. I cannot handle this much longer. Direct me to what you want me to do...and while you are at it, I added, could you bring me someone to live with me and help me make some corrections in myself instead of my always doing it for others?"

Now, if this were a movie, lightening would strike and the voice of my father would speak. No, sorry for you and me...this never occurred. What did occur, however, was the story that I told of the healers coming, etc. I did not get the connection right away but soon after Ivan Bakic came I realized... **WHEN YOU SINCERELY SURRENDER FROM YOUR HEART, EVEN IN DESPERATION, YOU ARE LIABLE TO CREATE WHAT YOU ASK FOR.**

In November of 1994 after working with my Reiki Master and taking treatments with him for almost two years, he initiated me as a Master. I was told by him that I must not go back to any other form of work. He said that Babaji has been very specific in his instructions for me. I was to do nothing but private Reiki sessions and Reiki classes. How, I thought at the time, will I ever get people to come to me or to classes because for one thing, most of Ivan's classes had come through the people I knew. But much to my surprise and happiness after Ivan went back to Croatia, which was in the fall of that year, I saw the possibilities.

I, as mentioned before, signed on for the Yogic Flying class and in December of 1994 completed that and came back to Connecticut.

By January of 1995 I was already being called to be seen for Reiki treatments. I have no idea how, but it was happening. In the same month I gave my first class. I remember the night before the class, lying in bed and thinking that I could not remember the how to say or make the master symbol necessary for initiating people. Oh, gadzooks! No one to call. What to do? Suddenly, it came to me as though I had always known it. Do I need to say anything about the relief I felt? The next day I would have to initiate 10 people. It was bad enough that I was unsure of my ability to make this even happen or that the students would feel anything but not to remember the main ingredient in the process was like forgetting to put the liquid in a sauce. Get the idea?

This was, then, the beginning of a long and wonderful series of Reiki classes, which continued until my mother had her stroke. I began to see private patients while continuing to keep my spiritual practice very active. I spent three hours a day with this practice and I was feeling truly alive and happy. Somehow I felt I had found my next niche. It was the most extraordinary path I had ever been on. I had opened and asked for a new way and sure enough a new paradigm shift presented itself.

In the meanwhile, we were receiving many signals to look for other housing and to prepare to move. This is a story all unto itself. I agreed to find and secure our place and Edgar Nentwig, my roommate for several years agreed to take care of the packing and moving. We began at least a year before the move, packing un-needed items and moving them into storage. Two brothers owned the building which was around 100 and some years old. A sort of Gothic Mansion with 12 unusual apartments. My apartment had been a music room and a salon of some kind which had a wrap around red tile porch off of the second bedroom. My room was in the turret and was semi-round with windows of stained glass and a floor to ceiling fireplace made of hand painted Chinese tiles, hand carved birds and a level of brass sculptures. This was all of the Chinoise period and I chose to make it my headboard.

Journey to the Center of the Self

The living room was completely hand carved oak with hand inlaid parquet floors throughout. It also had a walk in working fireplace.

When I first went to see it I was living in North Carolina. I entered and saw it as exactly my stage. It was another time in history and incredibly charming. I fell in love, offered the landlord a years rent, which he turned down. He did however give me a lesser price. I moved in as soon as possible and began reverse commuting to North Carolina. Après moi le deluge! (After me, the deluge!)

I lived there over sixteen years and now the time had come to move on. I found and asked Babaji to find us a place with lots of light, a great water view, etc. He gave me an apartment in New York. It was a triplex on Horatio Street which I rented from Sonia Trussardi, my wildly unusual Italian friend who insisted that I come there. My place was the second floor where I could see only the Hudson

River through large glass windows. It was full of light and perfect. The only problem was I did not want to live entirely in the city. So, along came the townhouse in Greenwich, Connecticut. I came into it to check the energy which seemed quite even and acceptable. It was in the woods, very light all the time with an atelier over looking the living room which would be perfect for my classes, etc. This was, of course, the beginning of a new story, did you expect anything less?

I had begun teaching my own classes in the city as well and when we moved into the townhouse in Greenwich I sat waiting for the furniture to arrive in what had seemed a very neutral energy environment. I sat up in the atelier on one foam "flying" mat. Nothing else had arrived yet and I thought I would meditate and do my flying program to balance and build the energy. As soon as I finished my program I found myself so dizzy. As in a whirl of energy and at once the entire place had changed from neutral to a very high vibration. Each thing that happened during those days was just another disbelief to believe. Does that make any sense to you? I mean sense within the context of my experience, of course.

The long and arduous task of unpacking, which I always have disliked, began until we were finally somewhat settled in our new modern and very brightly lit new abode.

Lisa Gengo had been with me for some years on and off. Some of those years were as a volunteer when I was Director of Friends of Children and she was taking a respite from serious work and had found employment from a clothing store which had agreed to give me their damaged (although it never really was much damaged) clothing for shipment to my programs in Guatemala, Honduras, Haiti, Thailand, New York and other places in the United States. Lisa's father had done some kind of helping work for Haiti and so she asked to help me as a volunteer. She was, therefore, present through my years with the NGO Childhope on who's Board of Directors I sat and through my travels to the countries where I supported programs for children. She joined some of my 75 volunteers at a later time, to work on benefit committees to raise money for charities.

This also meant that she was in my life at a time when the Croatians came. Prior to that time I supported her in her desire to return to school and later to move into and eventually buy a home for herself. Both she and Edgar accompanied me to Colombia, South America when I was invited to teach physicians at a medical school. They also joined me, although mostly Lisa, on my teaching trips through Southern Florida as well. By the time Lisa was initiated I took her with me to Malmo, Nebraska to learn the basics of a Hindu ritual performing puja and havan. This was a great spiritual time for us both and our Mahavatar teacher was most present in spirit all during that experience. Following this, we were invited back yet another time to teach Reiki on the same ashram (a Hindu monastery of sorts). My strongest memory of this occasion was the intensity of the energy and how Lisa literally became physically sick after the initiations, recouping herself with a bath and lie down. But of course I have gotten ahead of myself so let me take a small side moment and fill in for you the experience of Lisa's initiation as a working Reiki Master.

She wanted to be a Reiki Master and although I did not particularly want to be her master, Ivan Bakic said that I should be the one to teach her and guide her through her life until she worked out her differences with herself, her parents and me. In my case I am not sure she ever came to terms with me. However, I followed his instructions and eventually, although I felt it too early (for me the process would require at the very least, one year), I initiated her in April, as a Reiki Master and then convinced her and Edgar (who was already a TM mediator) to take the Yogic Flying course with me. I may have my timing a little reversed. I may have initiated her after we took the flying course. Yes, I am sure that is how it went. But then that does make you follow a little closer, no?

Actually, in thinking back, I remember the day of her initiation quite vividly. It was of course my first initiation of a master as well. We invited all the students that I had in my many classes with whom she had been present to join us at another students weekend house near Washington, Connecticut. The initiation took place on a very pleasant and calm day at a lovely home overlooking a beautiful river. The room was full and quiet. Everyone closed their eyes and I began. During the initiation a strong wind began to bang shutters in the house and yet when it was complete everything became quiet again. The

wind never was outside but only inside.
Don't ask me to explain that one because
I cannot. But none of us, and there were
many, ever forgot it.

We went on to several other
interesting adventurous investigations at
that time including seeing a
nutritionist/intuitive in Nebraska
followed by a Mr. David Slater who had
been the student of Hanna Kroeger, the
famous naturopathic nurse in Colorado
(that is famous to some of us) who was
known for her great healing powers, use
of herbs and other methods and many
books on the subject. We had signed up
for her summer class in Colorado but she
died a week or two before our going and
so we took the class with David Slater
who had developed some interesting
prayer waters for various and
multitudinous diseases. We studied and
tried his remedies for a few years but
neither of us could really say what we
felt were the results. He and his work,
however were and continue to be, most
fascinating and for some quite amazingly

helpful. He teaches in various parts of the world so is quite well known in some circles.

One of the greatest things that came out of that experience in Colorado was my meeting of a most brilliant woman, a Ms. Nina Murphy of New York City, with whom I eventually studied the same work as Slater as well as Peruvian Shaman work. I started her lecturing to a batch of my clients and students about the work of Hanna Kroeger and then about her work and extensive work with healing oils finally ending in her teaching of the mesa work of the Shaman. This included about twenty people ensconced in my living room putting down circles of tobacco and maize under a piece of material to be used as the alter which had first been cleared with a South American item know as Aqua de Florida. We then placed various pertinent objects in an appointed place on the altar (mesa) and began to learn the ancient chants, etc. Most fascinating although if I look at it as most of you will, quite an amusing and eccentric sight. But is this not part of what makes my life so interesting and this book so interesting to read?

I am only touching lightly on these subjects for exotic purposes as well as letting you in on some of the things that go on in the world that most of us never hear about and perhaps never wish they did even now.

Again, I am too excited and getting just a little ahead of my history. Allow me to explore with you the best of all of what has happened in the last seven or so years. During some of these times, and near the same time that Edgar and eventually Lisa went their various paths I met, first as a client and later a someone who in reality became a person perhaps, closer and more trusted by me than any other in my life. Her name was Winnie Staniford. We laugh to this day about how she sat in her car and waited until the exact time of her appointment with me. At the precise time (or so Her watch said) she rang my doorbell. I opened the door to a huge and highly evolved energy. Physically she was naturally blonde with huge, intense blue eyes and an incredible enthusiasm. "Hi, I'm Winnie Staniford" she said as she extended her hand. I shook it and jokingly said, "you're late, get in there". She entered and I directed her to my living room and a couch where we could sit together. She had come to have her astrological chart done with a particular focus on her business. When we were finished I asked her if she wanted a Reiki treatment which was what I really did for a living. She agreed. I did the ten-minute treatment. She said she felt great and that was that.

Winnie had been on her way to Italy at the time we met and as she reports "I felt so great for three months that I thought all I had to do was take a treatment once every three or four months and life will be good." After three months she made another appointment for a treatment. She came, took the treatment, talked about Reiki for a short while and went on her way. This time, as she likes to say, "I felt horribly depressed" and I thought "I can feel this way without paying for it". She called and we got together to talk. I explained about processing. That is, how the energy that one contains over issues of over a lifetime, feelings and thoughts and experiences, etc. must be released in a purification form that I call "processing". What goes in must come out. What we resist will persist. The issues are in the tissues. These all describe what goes on when we hold on to this and that throughout life.

Winnie stuck to me, as they say, like white on rice. She spent as much time as possible talking with me, asking questions and more questions and more questions. We shared life stories and found immediately that we reminded each other of our fathers. It took its time but faster and faster we began to know each other better and deeper than either of us had ever known anyone else. We both felt trust and a desire to tell all. Well, we probably held back a lot, but it seemed as though we were completely open. She heard all my stories and I hers. In between all of this I told her all the stories of my lifelong search for "IT". I explained that my only real goal was enlightenment. We talked about, in detail, everything I discuss in this book and in much finer detail. Well, to tell the truth, there is a lot of life that almost requires another book...in this case it took me years to tell it all to Winnie.

In Winnie I was fortunate that Nature had provided me with not only the best student I could have ever asked for, but probably the first real friend I ever felt was as good or better than what we would want in a family member. She took my Reiki I course followed it with initiation into TM and then Reiki II followed by the Yogic Flying course. In between she was growing and taking lots of Reiki treatments with me and working out a lifetime of confusion...a collection, as all of us, of childhood programming that led to self examination of her patterns, the energy work and finally her pursuit of surrender.

I was surprised when she came to me and asked to become a Reiki Master. Why surprised? Because being a selling artist of some stature, she could not understand how I could listen to people's troubles, work them out and then help them through the energy work. All to consuming to her at the time. Now, to my dismay, she wanted Mastership. If she were telling it she would say that it was one of the most difficult times in her life. A year of extremely deep self-examination and treatments and processing and purification. Brave woman that she was, she stuck it out and today is a prize of a Reiki Master. We work together during our classes and when I am lecturing.

The only other person that I initiated, as I said somewhere, was Lisa

Gengo. I knew her for many years and did as much as I could in helping her to really have a meaningful relationship with her family and with herself. With me, although I helped her along the way with **EVERYTHING** in her life, she always had some kind of a problem with my "sizzle" so to speak. Between her and my friend and roommate, Edgar Nentwig (who had helped me during the time of my car being burnt outside my home before a court negotiation. My ex-husband and his buddy were the natural suspects but in those cases not much can be proved.) we went to Florida and Columbia, South America where I had been invited by a physician's group to teach Reiki as an alternative. Lisa helped and Edgar helped me with my Spanish. His translations were much better than mine. If I had the time and space I could tell so many funny stories just about that. OK, one example. At the airport in Calle, one must go through so many checkpoints. Because of the drug war problems at that time there were enormous safety precautions in place. A group of poor and lovely people from Palmera, on whom I had done nearly free treatments, came in one old car to say good bye that early morning of our departure. Edgar had gone home a few days earlier and Lisa and I had gone through God only knows how many checks of baggage and papers, etc. There were many young soldiers with major gun power, which had always made me a bit tense since my work in Guatemala. At any rate, we preceded to our departure gate, which in this case was a small room with windows, almost all around. We could see the helicopters hovering all around the planes taking off to assure safety. At one moment, there were guards with dogs, not your normal vicious type but more an assortment of house dogs that you would want to go up and pet. They were, however, trained as well as their armed masters. They were scary. We sat tensely waiting for our departure notice. Suddenly a dog high tailed it over to sniff under my chair..."Oh my God!" I said to Lisa. "What could have gotten on our shoes, we would never or had never encountered any drugs. What are they looking for?" My heart was beating rapidly. Justice and jails are not what I was ready for. Just let me get on my plane and get out. Well, Lisa said "We can stop worrying; there is a piece of a donut under your chair." Good for a laugh and just one of many stories on just those kinds of trips alone. Another book I guess, although I am not sure I could face this again. I have had a life that feels as though it as been many, many, lives in one. Even my pictures change every so many years and it is hard for me to believe that this has all been me.

Prior to my meeting Winnie, I had gone with Lisa to Malmo, Nebraska to study a thing called Pujari work. That is studying under a person who works with the Hindu altar each day in a ritual of devotion going back centuries. We went to a Babaji (you remember him from the Croatian stories, no?) ashram there, first to study and some months later to initiate people in Reiki there. Very high energy, of course, and a wonderful experience. I might have mentioned that the vibrations were so high that Lisa had to leave and be sick to her stomach after the class. Another time of bringing Babaji's musician, Turkantam, who lived in France but had been with the Pujari in India when Baba was in the body. Turkantam was Baba's musician. He came and I gathered a group of 20 or 30 people in my house to hear him sing and learn with him the mantras and spiritual songs. This was a day of pure loveliness. I could feel the presence of my teacher in the room. This of course, was just one of the stories of that time. I went on with Angelo from the Malmo ashram to study "Jarah". I am unsure of the exact spelling, but it required many months of mantra repetition to build the energy to use 100 peacock feathers to cleanse the body of toxins of several kinds. You see, my search goes on and on and on. But I pray you will not experience it as such.

The funny story of that time was going to see the Dalai Lama to be initiated by him and listen to him teach for three days at the same time that I was using my mala (prayer) beads to keep count of the thousands of times that I had to repeat the mantra I have just mentioned. Well, many of the Tibetans were also doing mantra of some kind and using their mala beads as well. I was overweight and when one of the beautiful smiling women asked me what month I was in I thought she meant that I was pregnant and what month of pregnancy was I. No, indeed she was asking what month of my mantra counting I was in...we had quite a little laugh together and a few of the Tibetan women, whom I came to really love, had a great time together.

Following this period came a man that one of my clients, Angela Petrone, begged me to see. His name was David

Journey to the Center of the Self

Slater and he had worked with healing water and vibrations for many years with the Naturopathic Nurse, herbalist, and healer, Hanna Kroeger. I met him in Westchester, New York where he did his diagnosis techniques and began a regime that took many years. It also led me to take a series of classes offered each summer with Ms. Kroeger. About two weeks or less before the courses were to begin in Colorado, she died. Unfortunate for many and especially at that time for me. David Slater took over and Lisa Gengo and I went for a six day, twelve hour a day, seminar with him. This led me to one Nina Murphy who I heard constantly behind me asking and answering many interesting questions about something quite foreign to me. I loved her approach and knowledge mostly because I loved the way her senses and brain worked all together and so fast and funny. I sat in front of her every day with great pleasure. I describe this a few pages back, but these were the true feelings of our meeting. Although I lightly touched on this subject before, I wish to go deeper with my explanation.

Following this seminar I talked and wrote to Nina for at least three months convincing her finally to come out to my place and start teaching the ideas of Kroeger, Slater and the importance of scent oils. Her teaching was profound and yet completely sensible and based on solid ground. We all gathered a huge amount of knowledge from her, moving on with her to private sessions and using the Slater material as well as the many wonderful healing oils. It was Nina who was, and later studied more with her teacher in the Amazon, a Shaman. Indeed, she was the very one that I had invited to teach my students about laying the "mesa" and spreading the tobacco and maize in my living room. Remember? Well, I will never forget. Gadzooks! My inquiring never seems to end. But I am thankful because I can not only see my pattern but the pattern of how many different countries and peoples and ages come always or eventually to the same place although perhaps with a different name.

I HOPE YOU CAN SEE WHY IT IS IMPORTANT TO OPEN YOURSELF UP TO TRYING MANY THINGS WITHOUT TOO MUCH JUDGEMENT AND ALLOWING YOURSELF TO FOLLOW YOUR INNER VOICE. ALTHOUGH IT MAY LOOK AS THOUGH NOTHING IS CONNECTED, IN THE END, WHEN YOU STAND BACK WITHOUT JUDGEMENT AND EMOTION, YOU WILL SEE WHERE YOU HAVE COME TO AND HOW THAT JOURNEY ENSUED.

Going back to my story about the time I wanted to take a Tai Chi course and my root canal dentist recommended one Master Aston Hugh. A most unusual man indeed. Watching him do the "form" was like watching energy in motion, as in dance. He most probably was the best teacher I ever had. At any rate, I started going to one class a week. I suggested to Winnie who was spinning and running each day that perhaps a little quiet motion might be a good addition. She came to class and before you know it we were moving along like young Chinese kids. We went to class six days a week. Addicted now, to the movement of energy in a different way. There was no learning this martial art form with your intellectual mind because it was all muscle memory and when I turned off my thinking and just did the form I always learned it amazingly fast. We learned the first two forms and then he began a very small class of three of us to learn the sword form. We loved it. It fit so well together with the Reiki and the idea of moving the energy was so easy for us. Strange to say, I continue to this day to love the sword my Tai Chi Master gave me.

This, as you already can see, led me to the next interest, Chinese Medicine. The other student of mine I have made mention of, Lisa Gengo, had begun Naturopathic school and one of her school outings was a trip to Chinatown, in New York, to see the herbs, etc. used in Chinese Medicine. As was usual with her I had to dig out the information. Where did you go? Who did you see? What was the name of the most interesting place and practitioner? Finally pulling all of this out of her, Winnie and I decided to investigate. We found Fong at a special Chinese herbal shop in China Town where he did pulse diagnosis and then the teas were prescribed and made up for us. We saw him every other week for about a year in which we learned a lot about the diagnosis process as well as the use of herbs. So very similar to my experience with Ayurvedic Rasayana (Indian herbs). I suppose I will have to tell later about how I think they are so similar and why. For those who are devotees of the idea of reincarnation, it probably all goes back to some distant Chinese lifetime because it was VERY familiar and so easy to learn. You can only imagine what fruitcakes we were to others because, of course, we immersed ourselves into books on China and its foods and energy and way of thinking. I guess we became "pretend Chinese" for a few years. Well, Winnie and I have always been funny like that and I must say that before Winnie we were both investigative and immersive people in our own right.

Somewhere around the time of Nina Murphy, I had met a friend of hers by the name of Nancy Engel who was a colon therapist. Nina had said she was the absolute best and had been doing this and other very deep spiritual methods for over 35 years. I met her with Nina at a seminar of Gary Young Living Essential Oils. Some months later I had the idea that to do colonics would be a good way of "cleaning the pipes" as you would periodically do with your sink pipes. I tried a local place to find that it was much like a car wash. Cleansing, but not much more. I decided to try Nancy. Well, what a difference. She used a crystal over my head, which she could tune to the color of my choice. She had many singing bowls with which she could sound tones that fit with the color choice. She could tell exactly how you were eating and the condition of many organs of your body by observing your many releases.

Now I am most pretty sure that you are thinking oooooh, ouch, icky, how disgusting. Not at all. Very comfortable and very cleansing. I was beginning to feel much better and I could feel my whole insides responding. My moods changed as well, somewhat depending on which oils she used to massage my legs or back or stomach with to increase or assist my releases. She is quite an amazing woman with years and years of knowledge.

I was quite heavy at the time and had gone on diets, seen doctors, had tests and finally in a panic, gone to see an endocrinologist who was a research doctor in charge of a department at a large hospital. What a disaster. Pills, special diet and a huge amount of scare tactics. Results? Minor! I was not overeating and I was following, exactly what she advised but to little or no avail. I mentioned this to Nancy and she suggested a Dr. Terry Dulin. Well, I was more than fed up with doctors and had a fair amount of resistance to consulting yet another "EXPERT." Under the circumstances, however, I decided to call as a last ditch effort. I had been told that it took months to see him, but no matter. I called his office, spoke to the office manager who in turn told me that I would have a three or four month wait. "OK" I said, "but can you call me if you have a cancellation at any time. A moment's notice will do." Within one day she called and I spoke with Dr. Dulin. He was so fast and bright and charming that I felt completely comfortable with everything he had to say. It all made sense for the first time.

Of course I immediately told Winnie who had already been told by Nancy and she called as well. Both she and her father had suffered from severe headaches whenever there was a barometric pressure change. Of course no doctor ever really believed her so she had little hope. We both took complete blood tests and Dr. Dulin took very complete histories of each of us. He sees each person as a complete individual and as an Orthomolecular-Biolochemist, Naturopath, Nutritionist and Chiropractor he was in the perfect position to see everyone in their own cellular makeup. That is, he could (and still does) tell you exactly what you need to eat and what supplements you require to heal. He has examined varieties of supplements and has weeded out the ones he feels do not measure up to their labels. I found myself going through a series of deep toxic releases and only God knows how much I needed it. I did. As for Winnie, after following his regimen for only two months she was free of these awful headaches. True, she could no longer predict rain or snowstorms but she was entirely pain free. We have changed our programs many times but we continue after over four years to stick it out with this little genius. He can hear in your voice if you have been cheating a little here or there. We have found we cannot fool him and we only hurt ourselves. I lost 127 pounds without any assistance of appetite suppressants or the like, and many, many inches. I eat full and regular meals in a way that no one would be the wiser. This man has done more for me health-wise than anyone I have ever gone to. I use him, of course, in conjunction with my regular M.D. whom I like and respect very much but fortunately need very infrequently. My physician was amazed at how my vitals had changed and how fantastic I looked. He would, however, not even consider talking to Dr. Dulin. I find it most unfortunate that western medicine cannot make room for other possibilities in combination with itself. It could make such a difference to so many people. Somehow western medical doctors in general, excluding some who are more insightful, only look at alternative ways when they could be doing so much more. Although I was trained as a scientist I am always open to new or better methods. It has worked for me.

I am most happy to say that my search has not ended. I have certainly found myself in all of this. I would hope at almost 67 years old and all this searching and experimenting something would have come of it.....and it did....for sure.

The next adventure came when I decided to take a course called Vedic Literature and Human Physiology. It was there that I met the most miraculous Alarik Arenander, PhD. (He is the Director of the Brain Research Institute in Fairfield, Iowa and a phenomenal corporate speaker besides being a talented researcher.) He walked into the room where I sat with Winnie of course, and along with several others, none of whom I knew. I felt a deep feeling of joy and when he began to speak the knowledge, I was unsure if I could completely follow everything but I felt a deep assuring feeling that it did not matter. All I had to do was sit and let the knowledge and sounds penetrate my being and it would be understood. IT WAS.

To my complete amazement, and be sure I am cutting the story of these course days VERY short, I was so filled with understanding and such a high of complete freedom and joy that it is and always has remained both unexplainable and inexpressible. Talking about a kiss, which I usually say about my Reiki work, is disgusting, but experiencing it under most circumstances, most certainly is not. I will never be able to put into words the bliss I felt for five months following that course. I am forever grateful to Maharishi of TM fame as well as his messenger Alarik. I have continued to keep in touch with him and from time to time see him for an ice cream. We both love ice cream but he never seems to get fat from it. This, I must say, just does not seem fair. Of course he is also a meditator and Yogic Flyer.

One of the last things I got interested in through my friends Dr. Jay Glaser (he, by the way is a very well traditionally trained physician as well as an Ayurvedic doctor since the early seventies) and his wife Danielle, was going to Canada for training in Sanskrit recitation.

They told us there was a course in Canada a few summers ago and we decided to take the chance. My son Dante and his girlfriend of the time, a woman my mother totally adored, were willing to mother-sit for me for two days so we began the next hilarious trip.

We flew Jet Blue Airlines to Burlington, Vermont where we did our usual routine of laughing uncontrollably over nothing. I, tripping over my bag into a ladies room stall and Winnie standing by and laughing. I proceeded to the rental car counter as she went to fetch the baggage, our other routine besides laughing all the time...and who knows why? Once on our way to the garage for the car, we opened the trunk. She had a bad back so I wanted to lift the bags. I was "older" so she wanted to lift the bags. In all of this and all of the perusing laughter, we somehow realized that we had, most probably, left the keys in the trunk. Back inside we went. No, the only other keys were in Connecticut and our only solution was to drive half way around Burlington to get another key made. We did so and our drive into Canada began. We put the top down driving every now and again between some raindrops. Who cared? We were on our way to who knew where and we were free. The countryside was beautiful and the little towns so lovely and peaceful. Then came the border crossing. "Any drugs or firearms?" we were asked. I thought "what does she want to know next, do we have any bodies in the trunk?" The little villages were becoming smaller and less and less lovely but we proceeded.

We drove for about an hour or so until I saw the sign for the Auberge. Winnie kept driving. We were in total disbelief at the look of the place we were to stay for the next two nights. She kept driving. We were like Thelma and Louise because we came to the end of the road in a sudden screech and a lot of dust. In front of us was a small cliff. This was DEFINITELY the end of the road. Back we went. Begrudgingly we got our bags out of the car and looked for a valet or someone to carry our luggage. I asked someone and she said to just carry them up the million stairs in the rain ourselves. Great! Let the games begin!

Once there and settled in rooms across the hall from each other, we tried to settle ourselves. After all we were here on a serious learning trip. We found our way around the Auberge and found the schedule of events. Meditation, dinner (lots of vegetarian carbs, of course, but French and much too delicious). Then on to our way to the introduction of the course. Everyone so serious. What was with us?

Michel Angot has the unique background of both Western academic educations, earning his PhD in Sanskrit from the Sorbonne University, and many years of extensive training in the Pundit traditions of India. Angot has been teaching Sanskrit (Vedic and Brahmanical texts) at the Paris University since 1992. He is a specialist on Sanskrit grammar, Professor at the National Institute for Oriental Languages and Civilizations in France. That should have let us in on the clue that this was not to be taken lightly. In other words, no laughing. We were with people from many places in the world and as Monsieur Angot was French the class was translated into at least English if not one other language. It appeared he was an incredible teacher and we felt the need to settle in and pay close attention to his words and proper pronunciation of the chants.

What a time. We were in the lower part of this building, very French and I felt with the small windows with blue trim and the stone walls that I was at a meeting of the French resistance. This caused a very deep inner chuckle.

We listened and learned and chanted mantra and "flaked out". We did this all morning, through the afternoon and again in the evening after meditation and supper. I was so uncomfortable in the chair and my back and neck were becoming so tight, that I was forced to make a pillow out of my pocket book and lean way down in my seat. I chanted along as best I could, reading from the pages and listening to Angot until I was in some kind of altered state. Winnie said my eyes were half closed and my breathing quite slowed as in sleeping. I was not, just altered. This however, became the subject of constant humor and laughter as she continually imitated me much to my delight. We were getting a little higher in consciousness from the vibration of the mantras and the giddiness continued way after the evening classes into our room. We had, along the way, met Richard, a friend of the Glaser's and he appeared not to be able to leave us or to stop his laughing with us either.

On the day we left, we dragged our bags down the stairs, then on the grass, to our car. Richard followed us to our car and as Winnie gunned it out of the parking lot she yelled back at him "See ya kid!" This made more fun. "Winnie" I said, "you just called a fifty or sixty year old guy...kid." Well, we bring this up from time to time when we want a good memory. The course, however, was extremely powerful and well worth the trip. The information of how all languages are basically bastardizations of Sanskrit is fascinating and how some people thousands of years ago were able to access the sounds from the universe and understand their meanings is quite outrageous, no? He explained that this Sacred Sound was not just solely from India but was carried by these nomadic sages from, most probably Persia to what would be India to China, etc. and that is why there is so much of the same knowledge in these cultures. It is said that the Sanskrit word OM is the vibration that created the world as we know it. An interesting concept, I think. What about that?

This was the last of our trips for a long time because of my need to care for my mother for the next three or four years. Of course we took her to Miami for her 90th birthday and had a great time. We were asked to spiritually clear the space in a famous hotel. It had a terrible energy and we cleaned their offices and many of their guest rooms. That was certainly a "trip" in itself.

I would say that I have come to the end of the search for the miraculous, but it just would not be true. Things have come together now. I have taken all these seemingly disparate pieces and made them into quite an understandable whole for myself. Things make complete sense now and I am fortunate to be open enough to have made and continue to make large paradigm shifts in my consciousness. The best part is I am in a position to pass them on to others, which is my main desire.

Just last night I began to put a lot of my life's learning together in a grand scheme that I saw in the late sixties and I think I am finally going to be able to realize it's completion. Hopefully, in Iceland because of its lack of pollution and it's openness to innovative thinking. (More to be written on this subject.)

I am writing quite late into the wee hours tonight and I am hoping that I don't get any more bright memories for this chapter. My life has and is so continually full that all of the fun and pathos cannot be written in one book unless I called it War and Peace and as you know, that has been done.

IN SEARCH OF THE MIRACULOUS

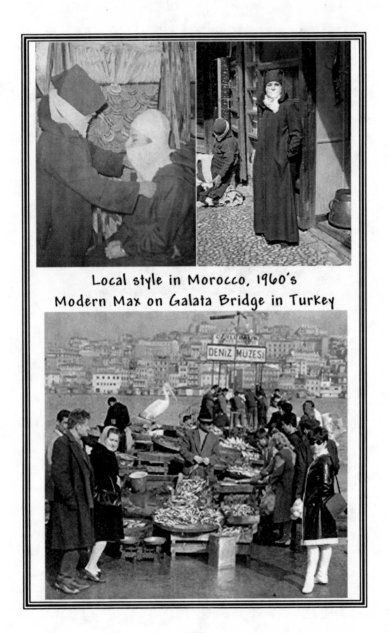

Local style in Morocco, 1960's
Modern Max on Galata Bridge in Turkey

Max in Florence, Italy, Rome at the Colosseum
Max in Athens near the Acropolis, 1960's

Arthur & Max, cruising to L.A.

Disneyland, and Niagra Falls
(more great photos by Arthur Gaudio)

Paco & Max in Acapulco, Mexico, with Sandra
at the helm on our way to L.A. 1960's

(below)
Max & Arthur at a family wedding 1960's

Max & Art at play
on land and at sea

Beatle and va va voom!

1960s La "Countessa" At Home

Aruna ->

Stages of Dante, with mom
and with Robert Thorne,
and with the bear

Journey to the Center of the Self

Robert Thorne & the family, skydiving

Down the runway with Max

below, with airport owners & friends

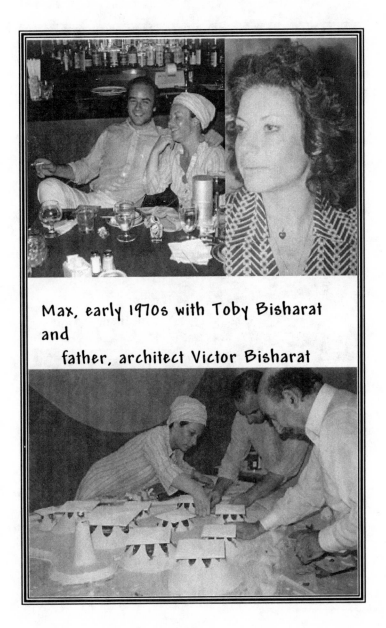

Max, early 1970s with Toby Bisharat and
    father, architect Victor Bisharat

Jiri, Max, Dir.
Friends of
Children, Edgar

Philip Swaim, my
divorce lawyer
of 17 years. He
died before the
case ended

Darling
Dr. Peter
Goodhue

Shiva Sharifzadeh,
daughter of Amir
and Shahla

My dear friends
the ayurvedic
physician Dr. Jay
Glaser, and his
all-wise wife
Danielle

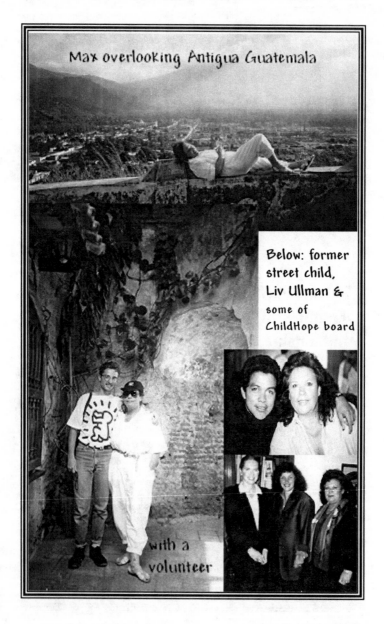

Max overlooking Antigua Guatemala

Below: former street child, Liv Ullman & some of ChildHope board

with a volunteer

Alvaro Arzu, Mayor of Guatemala City, later President of Guatemala giving Max an award for her work with street children there.

At my fundraiser for ChildHope at the U.N.

:hester (N.H.) — Sunday, June 14, 1987   15A

MARILYN ROCKY, left, and Max Gaudio, right, of Childhope tracked down $300,000... worth of medicine, convinced its owner to donate it, and got it shipped to Haiti for less than $300.
(Staff photos by Dick Morin)

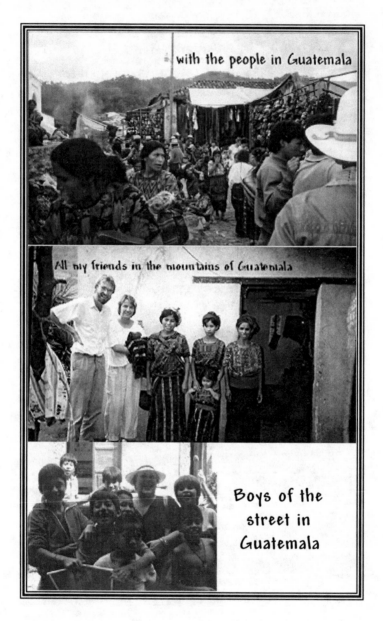

with the people in Guatemala

All my friends in the mountains of Guatemala

Boys of the
street in
Guatemala

Planning the work day, Haiti

Grueling work for Friends of Children

Delivering medical supplies at hospital Cite Soleil, Haiti

In the jeep on the dry riverbeds
leading to work in the pine forest, Haiti

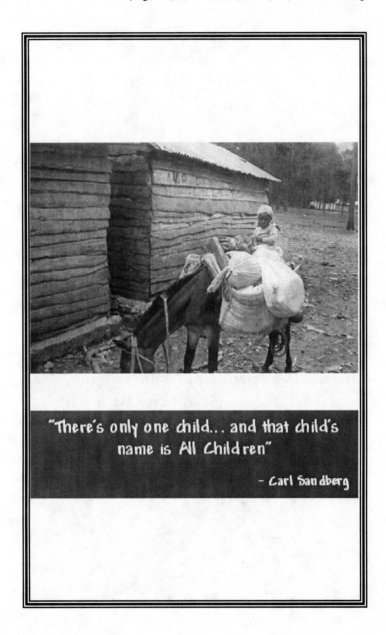

"There's only one child... and that child's
name is All Children"

- Carl Sandberg

Above, with Lisa Salerno, Amy Simon, AmeriCares volunteers on a night out with Max in Haiti

Below, with program directors who distributed Friends of Children's funds to feed 2,000 children per day in Haiti

Volunteer, Alex Auerspberg, Max, Ceil Ainsworth, Gil Donaldson, at my event for Victim Services

Tito Puente, Lolita Fonegra at Hot Night In Havana for Kids with Kids

The founder & the Board of Kids With Kids

My dearest friend Louis Branco who died at 40, before we had time to help more people and have more fun.

The spiritual players in the beginning of the school of energy work: Ivan Bakic (above) and Ivan Chuliac (below)

In my living room at Hackett Circle with Biba and Ivan, summer of 1993

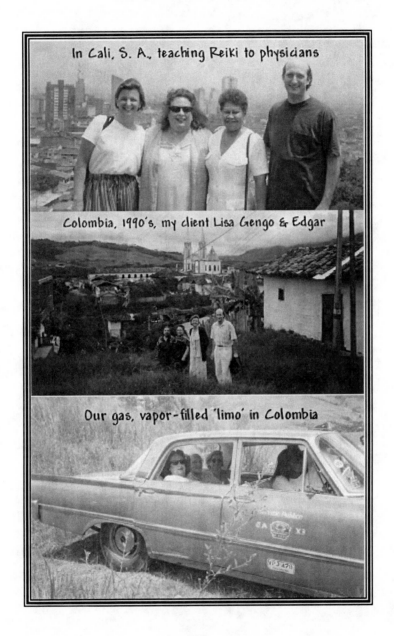

In Cali, S. A., teaching Reiki to physicians

Colombia, 1990's, my client Lisa Gengo & Edgar

Our gas, vapor-filled 'limo' in Colombia

"The world is a traveler's inn"

AFGHAN SAYING

Scottsdale AZ April 2006, relaxing
after making keynote speech for
Guardian Life Insurance.

Still in search of the

miraculous...

THE DISORIENT EXPRESS

I have learned to be that rare psychic surgeon who cuts through my own and others delusions to pinpoint the origin of a problem and help one begin to extricate from it. Whether it is uncontrollable behavior and addictions, unwanted thoughts or just persistently negative emotions, I get to the source of why we mess up our lives the way we do. Some problems can hold back or slowly negate a person over a chunk of life while other problems are really big explosions that reveal our issues. Divorce, addiction, criminal problems, health problems can all be wake-up calls to "get it together". But what about the more subtle lingering voices we hear that call us to lay down our weapons of "self-destruction" and go the way of the peace seeker? That hard to rid feeling that our lives are supposed to mean more than they do. How do we manage that inner turmoil and anguish that seeks bliss and connection with all living things? What makes me the phenomenon that some of my patients say that I am is that I am truly unafraid to immerse myself into the delicate and intricate small threads that weave together the ultimate fabric of our lives that makes up a human being's life.

It can be a very messy job as I have been known to say and I know this first hand as a spiritual warrior in the trenches of life, yet not entrenched by the drama and suffering of it all. Without attachment to the outcome, I have come to learn to offer laser-like logic searing through layers of atrophied, numbed-out psyches. I stick my neck out into risky places because I have taken so many other chances in my life that I seem to know I have nothing to lose and the

Divine most often allows me to see the "spiritual emergency" before me, whether it be an unhappy client who is depressed or a critically ill person who needs clarity and/or is near death.

Insightfully I am, in a way, a highly trained surgeon who extrapolates with great love, love from a greater place. From a distance I have been trained to use ancient symbols and high intention to send out healing energy to those I work on. The only fears that have been an issue in my work are the fears that other people have and helping them to overcome them. I see my patients get to that place of risk where they must surrender an old Identity in order to move forward. Though pain is a great teacher, the body and mind can actually get used to it and can actually fight change when one is looking to release old, outdated manners of living that don't serve our highest good anymore. Even when there is a paramount desire to change, surrender, move on and transcend, we panic because we feel like we are floating in an unknown sea without anything that is familiar for us to rely on. Like a drowning man clinging to a life jacket, even when the coast guard shows up to rescue us, we are often reluctant to release that life jacket, even when it becomes clearer that the very life jacket was actually drowning us.

Our instincts can often be detrimental when we seek to overcome obstacles on the path to self-realization. We are always deciding what we keep and what we throw out, and as we begin the process of releasing, surrendering and giving away, we open up to the magical flow of the celestial river. I have two feet planted firmly in the air as I beckon you to swim out to the deeper currents of the Divine River, which will carry one to a new place of understanding. Part of the instincts involves comforting our selves and medicating our incessant worries with food, sex, television, drugs, work, etc. We seek to numb ourselves from our pain because we somehow believe that it is too painful to sit with. Comforting ourselves is an innately positive attribute but when that comfort becomes a kind of escape, we would do well to observe ourselves as to what is happening.

We begin to see that numbing-out means we lose out on staying in the moment and witnessing our lives and the lives of those around us. As we begin to let go of control of our needs, etc. we begin to trust the Divine in whatever manner we believe in it. The point is that it is not us. As we begin to become conscious to our own nature to be addicted to suffering and we take steps to move beyond those needs, we realize how much of life in the world we have missed. We were so self-consumed with our own drama that we missed the miracles all around us.

I am a kind of worker of things that even to me are "miracles" trying to whip my dear clients into a better state of being with my hands and my heart. I am mostly unafraid to get down and dirty and be controversial. I say it like I see it is. The difference is that I do not waiver with my convictions. Comfort becomes an old blanket that we put aside and only perhaps need in emergencies, say when we had a bad day and give ourselves permission to have some ice cream. As we progress and become more experienced and are better able to handle life's stressors, we become less and less attached to our bodies and our egos. I like to say that I want to be permanently united with the Divine in everyday life.

Other people want a new house or car or more money or a new romance. We watch the way we get what we need and as we step further away from what we think we need we begin to laugh at the trivial tactics we employ to get our way. The body gets hungry so we feed it and doing so becomes a ritual of love and celebration. We eat to live not vice versa. As we begin this new journey on the path to our highest momentum we become privy to knowledge that seems to have been denied us previously. This new intelligence and higher wisdom is an affirmation that the universe is watching us and is pleased with our movement. I thrive on this energy and would be the first to say that this is where my ability to heal lies. I draw on the Universal life energy, chi, and quantum power. As I step out of my own shoes and into the divine flow of it all, I channel unconditional positive regard that the universe has for all it has created. It is that divine maternal swaddling that I make every attempt to bring to humanity like the great mother.

Though I biologically am a woman, my masculine side is very developed, making me well rounded and capable of reaching a wider audience. My appeal, some of my clients have said, spans from a homemaker to an entrepreneur a nurturer and an action-oriented mover and shaker. I stay on point as much as I can, with spiritual resolve and purpose that with the help of the Divine helps me to be unshakeable even as the earth quakes around me....It is, regrettably, not always the easiest thing to do (being as human as I am).

I have worked very hard over many, many years to be a source of stability in a seemingly chaotic world. 'Strange vibrations of other world charm emanate from me' says my friend Robert SanGiovanni. I feel both exotic and mundane, drawing on different times and different places, yet sometimes feeling timeless and placeless. My goal, plain and simple, is Enlightenment in this lifetime. Perhaps not for everyone but the only one that has interested me for much of my adult lifetime (sometimes I question the adult part, of course.)

Though I roll with the big dogs and have been know to have a pretty nasty bite when cornered, I am definitely no longer gripped up in the glamour of the "good life" that so many seek. People have struggles....that is what makes character and compassion. It can go the other way though, where people become nasty and bitter about what life has handed them. Though many seek to have material security, the old adage rings true that we must see beyond our insatiable desire for more to move to that place of unconquerable stability through any catastrophe...and all through history we have heard much of personal and group catastrophe, have we not?

For me, money is an energy that flows in and flows out just as we need. I trust that the universe will provide because as I have many times said, it always has. If you look in your life carefully..... look at the pattern, you will see that it is true in your life too...sometimes you have to look with a magnifying glass, but if you look you will see it. I have learned to ride through any storm, financial, emotional, physical neither attached to the outcome or the income.

There is a specific plan to each of our lives, and there is a special reason each of us is here, really, BELIEVE ME. When we meet others and connect it can become clearer that this is the universe leading us on a path to a new place. Teachers are put in our path, some amiable, some seemingly terrifying. Even those that cause us pain teach us and help us along our path. We recoil and tense up as we realize we just got burned by a fire. What we must recognize is that on some level we need to step into the fire in order to purify and destroy our illusions about what is pleasure, what is pain and what is immortal and everlasting. Robert has also been known to call me "The Queen of Detachment"...perhaps he forgot the part about LOVING detachment and well, perhaps it is true that I am capable of being truthful because I have lived it for many years. I have had times long ago when I lied, said things to make people happy, not faced the true reality of a situation but instead made it fit my belief or my romantic illusion or really what I wanted to believe to feel "OK". I have lived, worked hard for a long time to look for truths and be truthful to myself and others. I have been there consciously...aware of myself, there with every footstep, every heartbeat, every breath, with every word I speak.

I work hard all the time to be aware of my own divinity and my own greatness (most of the time, but I also have my moments) and I rely not on getting tempted by ego traps of power and self -congratulations. Accepting your own divinity and individual greatness leads you to the process of humility. Why? **Because if you do not feel really good about yourself you cannot be truly humble.**

For me, spirituality is the vehicle that gets one to that high place of detachment and great love and connection with all living things. To be detached does not mean to not feel or to be cold. It is loving and compassionate but not attached because the great

Journey to the Center of the Self

Buddha said "attachment is pain". I feel that whatever it takes to get you there doesn't matter....Whatever vehicle gets you there is great, just don't forget to get off the vehicle when you get to where you are going. Love can conquer all traps and entanglements that ensnare us. For me, world peace exists when we are together in that high place....and that means in relationships with others as well as with ourselves....Wars would not occur if we could all live in that consciousness. Great love is a pyramid, an offering to the Divine stretching wide across the plain as a symbol of gratitude to the universe and respect for life. We are the Gods and Goddesses and we rise above with our love. We raise each other to the sky in praise to show the world, that which is beautiful and right. Great love goes anywhere and finds itself in anything so that it can survive. Love creates itself over great stretches of time and space so that it can transcend. Love has to transcend if it will survive. It has to get to that high place so that the great nurturing and healing can occur.

The sacred water has to be given and received. Water heals and fire burns. We are clarified and burnished into our higher conscious selves through great love as impurities bubble over and our insecurities melt into nothing. We love each other but we are not addicted to each other. I love and it comes from my heart. My favorite boyfriend of all times once said to me "I see us dancing through the centuries, changing sexes, changing roles, but always together. There is no need to speak, for you do so without words." and I feel that way now about most people that are close to me including those that I have as close clients and those that I initiate in Reiki.

I have and sometimes continue to be surrounded by celebrities and debutantes (a few dilettantes too, if I must say) and yet I make a strong attempt at remaining unmoved by any status symbol. Some may call it the "Get

High Society", where people throw parties for other people to attend. A self-perpetuating faux high society that needs its own mirrors to exist. I was one of them until I decided to seek entry into the "Get Higher Consciousness Society". Our attachments to ourselves and to our expectations about others and ourselves lead to pain. The whole cycle of having it and losing it is like a train called "**THE DISORIENT EXPRESS.**"

A dysfunctional, runaway train, we clamor for more and yet never have enough to fill the hole that we have become. Like "Cellular Phonies," we have countless toys that make us look "cool" and feel smart and yet we grow bored of these and tired of them. Once we get into the engine room of our train-wrecked lives, we can begin to change the course of our lives for the better. The Disorient Express can become orientated to us once we get on the right track. It can lead us down a tunnel to a new destiny. The train ride becomes a rite of passage. We are no longer watching life pass us by, but active participants in our own destiny. We are making the path as we walk it.

This last paragraph is worth taking note of even if it does not seem at first glance to be noteworthy because with knowledge we will no longer project into the future and past but we will **BE HERE NOW**, and what could be more important than that? If we live in the past we are eating yesterday's meal and if we live in the future we are eating tomorrow's meal. When this occurs we miss the meal in front of us.

Motto of the Social Ethic

The healing social life is only found when in the mirror of each human soul the whole community finds its reflection and when in the community the virtue of each one is living.

RUDOLF STEINER

*"You cannot travel the path until you
have become the path"*

GAUTAM BUDDHA

*"I stood at a crossroads and fate came
to meet me"*

LIZ GREENE

THE UNAVAILABLE PARENT

I have a theory I call The Unavailable Parent. This theory has culminated after years working directly with people from all walks of life, every conceivable situation and economic background and coming from every corner of the earth. I also developed this theory after years of observing myself, self-examination on the mostly intricate level.

In all my major love relationships, there was always something. I have come to believe that we all have one parent who was emotionally unavailable to us in childhood, and this parent frequently acts as an obstacle to actualizing our true potential. I also know now that whatever issues that parents do not deal with in their own lives, what they hide even in their subconscious, the children will automatically, psychically pick up on, try to fix and resolve.

In my own case, I thought my father was my Unavailable Parent. He was a brilliant scientist, but he was critical and tended to look at the world in only one way. It wasn't until I was an adult that I realized that my mother was my Unavailable Parent. Her powerful sense of judgment and fear of financial insecurity had a much stronger pull than what I had imagined. It pulled me into two bad marriages and a disastrous move to North Carolina with my young son.

Later, when I began to learn about Reiki and energy transfer, I realized that my mother was never emotionally available to me in the way I needed her to be. Without knowing it, I was making choices based on my desire to have what I missed as a child. Why? Because as children, we all want our parents to nourish and sustain us, and when they don't it's unbearable. Regardless of the details of how it played out, it is our perceptions of what went down that left an indelible negative mark on our psyches.

It is imperative that as adults we identify The Unavailable Parent and free ourselves from that bondage. Ask yourself, "Which of my parents am I more like? Who was the one that I feel I did not get? Am I currently still trying to get it?" I help people do this all the time, not by changing their circumstances but by helping them to clear the path for circumstances to change. When they change, and drop the need to fix or alter others, all sorts of remarkable things occur. Today I have come to understand my relationship with my son and have made peace with my ex-husbands. And talk about a full circle of change, The Unavailable Parent---my now 93 year old mother, Doris---came to live with me at the age of 88 when she could no longer live on her own. What was inspiring to see is that we came to get along so nicely.

Once one deals with The Unavailable Parent issue, their energy can flow freely and they are finally free to do or be anything they want. It doesn't matter how old you are, how many jobs you have had or how many divorces. The real telltale factor is how you really feel inside when you are alone sitting with yourself.

Let me digress (once again) just for a moment to show you a dialogue between two people that spans over a time period of 12 years. Here is a window into what two people were thinking, what attracted them to each other, how it grew into an incredible life altering, high-consciousness connection and alliance. Watch this movie as it transpires.

Invariably, because of the subconscious core feelings left from the legacy of The Unavailable Parent, you subconsciously pick the unavailable parent, even if they do not look or act that way. Looking deeper you will notice the connection and see the pattern of your life. If you were beaten, you may be attracted to beaters. You do not want to be beaten but it is so familiar on a subconscious level. You want that perceived unavailable parent to be available. The kick or the high that you are seeking is the acceptance and love of what you perceived from the unavailable parent.

In 1992, I was doing a fundraising event in NYC for a charity I had founded called Kids With Kids, Inc. and I was contacted by a friend who had seen and had a video of a performance group. He desperately wanted me to see this group. I saw the video and was interested in meeting with them. There were two main performers, Zu and Atom who had formed a group called Primatec. They were very unusual and very talented. As a matter of fact I recently made contact with them after many years and I am happy to say that Zu appears to have grown in stature and talent. He now has a show in California and a fabulous CD called Zu Human. At any rate, when they came to my house for the second meeting they brought the third member of the group, a 26 year-old man, who immediately reminded me of a photograph of my dad at the same age. It was uncanny how exact his profile, his hairline matched and he had the same name, Robert. He had the brilliance, the creativity and he immediately became wildly taken by me. "Please marry me, you're beautiful," he said right away. I felt, "What is it with this guy," I was 52 at the time and I was not interested in any attraction, strange or normal. I just wanted to complete my Kids With Kids project.

I began to see that he really responded to me and was deeply enamored with my vision. He came to New York where I worked as a Director of Information and Development for a private social service agency. He expressed a desire to assist me with the event even though his band ended up separating and choosing to disband. Not long after, he had a choice of returning to his home in Maine or staying with me to complete this project. We decided that at least temporarily, living and working together would be the best of solutions.

We had so much. He was so protective and nurturing while at the same time hilariously child-like. It was the perfect combination for me. We would stay up late into the night doing all sorts of fantastic dream-like things because he was able to translate my ideas into written reality. During the day, he was very good at assisting, almost cloning himself into me to help. He was one of the most talented loose cannons I had ever met. I had no intention of having any lover let alone him, but somehow we were so connected, so on the same consciousness that we barely had to speak sometimes. He anticipated any needs at exactly the right time unasked.

He was a romantic, passionate about life like me and he inspired me really deeply and made me feel as though for the one time in my life, after so many relationships, I could really be with someone on all levels at the same time, without any distractions or barriers. No need to withhold the intensity of my personality. No need to suppress my child-like nature, the dreams and fantasies or hold back the enormity of my intellect. What a combo, what a possibility. Searching my lifetime for someone with whom I could spiritually dance. So connected that we dreamt the same dreams.

From his part, (which he explained at the time of this writing) he had been smitten by a woman whose character he was sure he could never find elsewhere. In her eyes he said, "he saw the answer to all the problems of the world and he felt drawn in as if he was a knight

questing for the Holy Grail, her heart".
He said that he inwardly trembled at the
chance, an opportunity of such great
magnitude. To love one and to be
consumed but brought higher and in the
process bring her with him. He said that
he trusted her like he had never trusted
and he was not completely sure why. He
had reason to believe that the Gods were
at play; something extraordinary, beyond
their immediate comprehension was at
work.

Although he saw all this and more,
it was all he could do to sustain an
emotional connection. Because his
self-esteem was so low, hidden under a
lot of fabrications, it slowly worked its
way into their connection to undermine
his faith in himself and his ability to
succeed. Unfortunately he was trying to
succeed for her and live up to what he
perceived as her expectations of him.

He began to see her as his father
who had shamed and emotionally
threatened him and most of all would

never acknowledge his genius and therefore his uniqueness. And so the struggle began.

She observed that while he had terrific bouts of joy, exuberance and productivity, he was also susceptible to serious depression and changeability. His inner child, who never completely resolved the issue left from the Unavailable Parent, either threw a temper tantrum or scowled and brooded, running away to a safe place. Fear made him want to fight or flight, but at that stage of his development, he may not have had the tools to fix it. He could go out for a run lovingly saying goodbye and return a completely different person in a dark mood that was contentious and blaming.

It would come to pass that his mood-swings were reckless and although he wanted the relationship with her more than anything, he consistently undermined himself knowing that he would ruin the possibilities for keeping this beautiful relationship whole and in its full glory. He was afraid he couldn't live up to what he thought she expected of him and what he originally proclaimed himself to be.

She on the other hand, was hurt and baffled. She was giving everything. She respected him and admired his talent. She nurtured him and fed him emotionally and physically. It was her main desire to set him on the path to his success. However, her issue was about her Mother who promised everything and gave little of what was promised leaving her with issues of trust. She did not know whom she was dealing with from moment to moment or what to believe. The dilemma ensued; a terrible attraction coupled with colossal disappointment and betrayal just as it was with her Mother.

What made the emotions so difficult was his inability to keep his word. This was more important than anything to her. It had to be the foundation of an honest loving relationship. This was a great possibility of joint accomplishment for the human good. He wavered with his love and she saw that he really did want to love her and this is part of her disillusionment. She wanted so badly for him to get over his issues which were clearly keeping him disconnected from his power, but she also saw that he was capable of being there for her and wouldn't. Why?

Their relations did indeed become strained, the feelings of love turned to suspicion and mistrust. She saw that he was making her into his unavailable father, releasing his fear and rage onto her and punishing her by knowingly playing into her Mother issues. All her kindness was spit back in her face. She tried over and over again by talking and explaining and sitting with him. At times, he would beg for mercy and she saw that he at times was very clear and capable of grasping what dynamics were at play. He would admit that he was projecting and he would be able to rise up temporarily.

He understood very well that their combined talents could bring great change into the world community. She wanted him to get over this stuff and perhaps in a different time and place they could have weathered the storm but that was not to be at least not right away.

No matter how much they both wanted the other to be what they never got as children, it wouldn't work. They each had to focus on their own inner work and want to for their own well-being, not just because the other wanted them to. If they could stay together to work through the crap that came up after the euphoria of the honeymoon wore off, all the better because they would be cleaning up the Karma they incurred.

Finally though, she had to draw a line and say, "Connect or leave. " It quite possibly ripped her heart in two to have to make this order but she inwardly knew that she must. Although she wanted to help him she realized it was at her expense. He resented the perceived power imbalance that he had with her and he somehow always wanted to reckon that by pulling her down and sabotaging moments of goodness.

Although he tried desperately to pull all his disparate pieces together, to make good on his promises and the love he felt, he ultimately was forced to leave her in a moment of quiet desperation.

Of course that was not to be the end of their story, but years passed before they would connect. She always kept the door open for him for she knew what an important relationship it had been for him. She assisted him at times when he was in crisis and he again made deliberations as if he was finally getting it and was ready to be what he had originally represented himself to be. From a distance, she watched his games and was consistent in her caring but she was now fully immersed on her own path of self-realization and spiritual enlightenment.

While he slept in a homeless shelter and de-toxed off marijuana and alcohol, she met a Reiki Master from Croatia who would change her life. She had a decision. One weekend he wanted to see her as he had just left a rehab. He struggled with his desire to go and his fear of going. She had to sit with whether or not it was productive or just another ploy. She made the choice that that weekend she would have the Reiki Master as a guest rather than submit herself to more of his instability.

He went his way and followed what he thought was his path which in hindsight was nothing but a variation on the same old theme. He would call her and ask to be rescued and she helped but he never seemed to get over his stuff or get stable. He bounced from job to job and couldn't stay in one place for very long. He had successes but didn't seem to really make big changes.

As she progressed on her path, magnetizing what she wanted, it was clear that she released any debt she felt she owed him. She never disconnected entirely but she distanced herself because for her it was over, or so she thought.

Years later, perhaps five or six, he contacted her. He had now married with one child and one on the way. He wanted to visit her and she invited him and his wife to come. She was pregnant and did not want to travel or be alone without him. She had taken on the role of his Unavailable Parent (His Father) and he was unwilling to incur her wrath. Once again he promised and reneged. Later he did come with his one daughter for the weekend and had a good reunion.

The old sparks were still there even though he was in a marriage that was not feeding him the way he thought he wanted to be. He was studying massage therapy, and she offered to initiate him in Reiki. Relishing his longtime connection with her, he was happy to reconnect with her in a positive way. All seemed well and she invited his wife to come and take the first Reiki course to which she agreed. The two women had a good time talking about what difficulties there were in a relationship with him. Apparently nothing much had changed.

After a ninety-day period, it was appropriate for him to be initiated in Reiki II. He was excited about the possibilities of being able to heal energetically and his demeanor and sincerity encouraged her. He asked if he could cover his expenses by massaging some of her clients and she agreed. He was able to sustain himself but not enough that she felt comfortable initiating him. She was concerned that he was not mature enough to handle the responsibility that went with using the Reiki symbols and how he could effect change. She ultimately declined to proceed because in the face of all the processing he was doing, he got very angry and in a fit of rage, mentally envisioned how he could physical hurt her. She was bringing out his Father issues so succinctly that he literally exploded with the possibility of a dangerous outcome.

What he didn't see was that he was purifying and that his father issues were coming out and that he was once again projecting them onto her. She again was very disappointed but asked him to leave and stood her ground. He left confused at his own inability, and really unable to see clearly that it was HIS STUFF. She was hurt that she had offered such profound tools for healing only to have him bite the hand that was nourishing him.

Then years again passed and she did not hear from him except occasionally when he was in a good way. Invariably, he would always lose the connection even though she saw him capable of such intense honesty, clarity and ability to be a great healer. She hoped for the best but detached from him. He slowly began to mature as the role of being a father finally pushed his addictions into submission. He quit smoking and drinking again and was able to STAY sober. He began to address his mood swings and sought help through his diet, exercise and therapy. He began to process more and more and release the inner demon of hate that had poisoned his life and sabotaged any progress he made.

He gradually started to forgive his father and realized that his father had taught him much. He began to take his weaknesses and turn them into strengths. He eventually contacted her, as this was, he said, his ultimate desire, to return to the great teacher she was for him and fulfill their combined destinies creating the possibilities of which they had always dreamed. He saw such deep gentle compassion in her eyes, as he always had, that he decided to forever bury the sword and lay down his arms to be in hers, united for a greater cause of peace for humanity.

He had cleaned up his life and become a man. He put away the fantasy of being a boy and being accepted by his dad and when he did he became a better man than most. He was eager to face responsibilities even now with a third child and yet a pending divorce. He realized that even now he must relieve himself of the burden of trying to fix a dysfunctional marriage (based on his father). He let his wife go to be her own person and make her own choices, right or wrong.

He began to see his children in a new light especially the one that reminded him of his wife and therefore his father. He was still seeking approval from his eldest daughter and she was only 10. How insidious our subconscious way of doing things, how we begin the negative pattern on a whole new generation only for them to pick up the broken pieces and go out and replay themselves in their own way. So now for him the movie had reached a pinnacle point of full circle relevance in that he was who he had always wanted to be and whom she knew he was always capable.

For her, she had reached a whole new level of consciousness. Her dedication to her path and her zeal for the well-being of others had culminated now in the merging of her knowledge and the opening of her heart for healing. While she had spent many years catering to the many that she felt obliged to fix or to repair or to help as though it were noblesse oblige. And then she said, "I quit; I can only change the world by changing myself."

She had garnered serious respect in her field and was now in a position to push her theories in a new direction to reach a broader audience at whatever level they were capable of receiving it. She wanted to write the memoirs of her life, and she as a common person went from a regular life with regular problems to a deep understanding of what was going on and the combination of techniques to overcome it. She wanted to convey this to others, how she went from A to Z, by showing what led her on her path to become a free person.

She began to write her book and in new conversations with him, they agreed to attempt to reconvene to collaborate on this writing project (they always wrote well together and she always regarded him as a fine expresser of her ideas.) She invited the idea of him rejoining her once again to see if this project was possible together and given their volatile history, she was fairly detached as to its outcome. She already had a man with whom she was writing but he had little concept of her or her deep ideas although he had the proper background and skills to accomplish what she was after.

Still, she always felt, "If only I could get my old companion, who had helped me with Kids With Kids. He was so fantastic and he could really finish my sentences and translate my ideas onto paper in a way that was timely, accurate and in the best language possible to express my feelings." He communicated with her that he had progressed and polished up his life and was interested in joining her. They made arrangements for him to spend a week with her to see how productive and fruitful the collaboration would be. He made the journey, neither of them with any other agenda than writing, but as soon as he came off the train and they embraced after so many years, their dance began immediately as though it had never ended.

Their time together began as cordial and hospitable but that very quickly led to what had originally brought them together. A great connection that was both emotional and intellectual. The old surge of deep love and affection coupled with harmony and understanding permeated the atmosphere of her home where they typed and talked, laughed and exchanged. Productive like there was no tomorrow, (their usual fashion); their time was to be a pursuit of happiness.

At a moment one afternoon, he momentarily felt an old demon arising, as his mind raced and a familiar fear seized but for a few seconds. He perceived a loss of his power and immediately transferred that anguish onto her as though once again she was the powerful one, his Father. He felt like he was succeeding and he panicked and turned his angst on her, making her the object of his insecurities. Their old battle began but this time it was different.

He rather quickly retrieved himself and was able to maintain a modicum of calm. He recognized his demon and admitted what was really going on. She refused the battle and he owned his aggression and his attempt of transference onto her. Although she knew intuitively that he was in terrible pain, she held her ground and gave him the choice of being peaceful and resolving this or leaving with a chasm all too familiar to both of them.

He said to her, "Don't you know how powerful you are?" and she replied, "Don't you know how powerful YOU are?" They sat down together and he calmed down and looked at her sitting with her orange jacket on and what he called her "Nerdy" leopard glasses. He exclaimed, "What is wrong with me? I am sitting with a living guru who is really only here to benefit me and I want to make it into a battle where someone wins and someone has to die."

She asked him tenderly, "What is it that you really want?" He pondered this question for a few moments, and blurted out, "I want my father to love me," as he cried emphatically in her arms. In that moment he made the decision to stop what might have been many lifetimes of warring on the battlefield with each other. He got it. He no longer wished to try and win because he realized that carnage had always been their ending.

Now was their opportunity to heal and transcend. Thus, their merging brought forth the purpose that was intended for them many years ago. The child they were now to create together, the birthing they would usher into the world could be a brand new way for many people to connect, a place for real, lasting peace to begin, between two individuals. Healing together, these two would combine their awesome energies to heal each other and send forth their unison into the universe.

Chivalrous and transcendent, their love for each other burned not for either of them and this they knew implicitly. They realized that their love was something bigger than each of them and for something bigger than them. There was an excruciating beautifulness to their connection for there was no selfishness to their wants of each other, and there was freedom and full acceptance to be who ever each other wanted to be with no strings attached. The garden of their love was in full bloom and the seeds of a grand future had been planted.

Now she had found a companion and collaborator who could assist her professionally and support her emotionally. He had surrendered his old need to fight her, turning around his destructive ways to benefit his career and win a great love of his lifetime. In her he found completion and a mirroring of a great mind. In him she found boundless exuberance and an equally great mind that matched her own. Thus they realized that world peace could exist when they were in that high place together and peace existed between them. If two people cannot manage their relations, how can the world? World wars would not occur if individuals stopped being at war with each other. Whether it be their spouses, their siblings, their children, their parents, their co-workers, their bosses or their neighbors, global harmony like charity, begins at home.

Their love was like a pyramid stretching wide across the plain as an altar to the deities. Their love could go anywhere and find itself in anything so that it could survive. It creates itself over great times and great distances so that it can transcend. They realized that they were the gods and goddesses and that they could rise above, raising each other to the sky to show the world what beauty is. Their love has to transcend if it will survive. It has to get to that high place so that the great nurturing can occur and for them it had happened. They envisioned each other dancing together through the centuries, changing sexes and changing roles, but always together.

They spoke without words. She was the water and he was the boat rowing over her. He stopped rowing to feel the gentle ripples of her ease his mind.

They loved each other but they were not addicted to each other. It is okay to desire but they owe it to themselves as we all do to be there to clean up the wreckage of our pleasure rides. True love, love that goes beyond a powerful momentary kiss or the heroin-like hoopla of courtship through to honeymoon, is a myth to most of us; an unknown that we think will happen if someone (our mate) will just love us more. Always looking for the other to fulfill.

Resentment can happen when expectations get involved and we clamor for something that is perhaps unrealistic. What we are missing is that we first must love ourselves, without any attachment to others. IT IS realistic not to base our happiness on what another does good or bad. No expectations of reciprocity. True love is transcendent of any need or fulfillment.

We always think that love is a hunger that can never be fed or satiated; a gasping for air that can never be breathed; a thirst for water that can never be quenched. Real love is beyond the need for food, air or water.

Kahlil Gibran, in his book, The Prophet, states, "Love gives not but itself and takes not but from itself. Love possesses not nor would it be possessed; for love is sufficient unto love. Love has no other desire but to fulfill itself." And I say, is not the foundation of all religions and all spiritual teachings LOVE?

Thus the motto of this movie is that if people really want to see the truth and change, they to must do the work. They must find their pattern and how their perceived Unavailable Parent formed those perceptions. They must release their core pain through energy work and surrender to whatever they consider to be the Divine; whether it be an orange, a tree, a flower, or a sunset.

IF WE GET WHAT WE SEEK, THAT'S GREAT. IF WE DON'T GET WHAT WE SEEK, THAT'S GREAT TOO BECAUSE THAT IS WHAT SURRENDER MEANS.

Most often we will find that when we surrender and do not actually get what we set out to do or wished for, we find something much bigger and more rewarding. Perhaps we find something that sends us in a new direction previously unthought-of or a path of better personal growth.

Robert & Max

"Be not a flower in a fool's buttonhole"

RABINDRANATH TAGORE

CHANGING SEATS ON THE TITANIC

Changing seats on the Titanic is a common way (to some who are seriously addictive) of saying that a person is changing addictions. I have mentioned in many chapters that until you find your "baggage" and work it out, you will most probably, depending somewhat, perhaps, on your brain chemistry, feel an unbelievably uncomfortable and yet deeply imbedded, pain. In many cases we tend to cover up these feelings by finding something to relieve the pain. To push it down....way down. Some of the ways of doing this are alcohol, drugs, sex, smoking, work, falling in love <u>often</u>, going to the gym, food, and many other things... not just in a small way but in an addictive way. In the way that one feels compelled to "partake" in something just to feel better. Or in a "just one more time" way.

Many of these things are socially acceptable. Let's go grab a beer after work, I cannot miss my time at the gym, got to go sneak just one cigarette, I just think I will break my diet, but only today....sure, the cake will never be eaten again, just today. When we give up one strong desire it is often followed with substituting another, ergo changing seats on the Titanic. Whatever we are doing that is destructive to our growth is not unlike being on a sinking ship.

This chapter will probably be short but meaningful because I will tell you some stories of my work with people trying to overcome something. In most cases the people who come to me feel desperate although I always wish that they would come with the desire to find their path and stick it out through the turmoil and pain, which with me, will be neither easy nor always pleasant. It will, however, be truthful, cutting to the quick, and not take years. This work with me can be done with me alone or in conjunction with your doctor or therapist, no matter, either as a "jump start" or a journey unto itself. Under any circumstances, if the individual wants to get better or change or get onto or stay on a spiritual path they WILL succeed.

Energy work is a powerful tool. Trust me, even if you don't want to.

Some cannot make the walk through the fire. I tell them that I can walk along side of them but I cannot walk their walk. I sometimes liken myself to a gas station. Some need their windshield cleaned, some gas, some just a road map while others need an entire valve and carbon job.

Fat used to be acceptable because society set that standard. There was a time when you couldn't be thin because it meant you were poverty stricken, being fat meant you had money. I think of my son at a "certain age" when I asked him if he found someone attractive. His reply was "no, she has a bit of a butt on her". This is just the most ridiculous. This thinking did not come from me nor did it come from his father. It definitely came from societal thinking, his friends and people, magazines, whatever. And how did that start, because some designers decided we should all look like that?

That is my point. Nobody thought it out. Many people never think anything out for themselves.

So if it's bad to be drunk you hide your drunkenness, if it's bad to be fat you try to hide your fatness. If you think you are too thin (which is quite unlikely in today's world) you think there's something wrong with you. If you have acne you might think you were ugly, if your nose is like this or that it's no good. If your old and your neck is getting wrinkled (oh, my gosh, I relate to that) you think you are old AND ugly (not me,

I like the idea of being older and wiser it is much easier). By who's standard? Not many think it out. Then you think about what you want but is it your want or did it come from your family, friends or society and what you were programmed to want? Not many sit down and say, "you know what, I don't want that". But they know they are not happy, they may not think it until the next day, but unhappy because they don't have what the guy next door tells them they should have or be. What the society is telling them they should have or should not.

Ok, but let's take it back a step, let's say your talking, let's just stay within the context of what you learned from your parents, what you picked up from your teachers. You're not getting where you want to go, what do you do?

How do you fix that? How do you kill the pain? How do you fix it, this is the point of the process.

Ahhh, how do you fix it? You have to really make an honest assessment of yourself and you may need someone like me to help you do that. *Honest*, you have to sit down and you have to be willing to face the crap that it's not someone else's fault, including your own perceived unavailable parent. It's nobody's fault. It is what has happened and it's how are you going to change it. But it's how are you going to change something you can't see. 'I don't understand, so how am I going to see it?' So if you think you are just an unattractive person how do you change that? You have to change your self-esteem, but how? How do you do that? Well you have to start thinking, what is the standard I'm trying to live up to? Then you have to look around for maybe, some kind of therapy or whatever it takes. In order to understand why you became this way. Then you have to go for some kind of energy work because it has to be worked out to feel joy and love and happiness, particularly about yourself.

Finally, and most importantly, it is of tantamount importance to find something, anything that you consider the Divine, and SURRENDER to it. I know that I say this over and over but not much else is important. **Truth-Simplicity-Love** all start on their highest level with SURRENDER. **Stop the never-ending static in your head so you can receive the broadcast.**

Both being loved and loving are, after all, probably the most important priority for us all from the very beginning until the very end and on a higher consciousness connecting with the love of whatever you consider Divine.

There are scientists working on research to prove that there are very strong links between love and health, happiness and inner peace. It will, more than likely, show how empathy, connectedness, compassion all have a direct important correlation to our mental, physical and spiritual well-being and possibly to longevity as well. Science is beginning to come together with more currently unproven yet believed concepts to show what ancient Indian, Chinese, etc. cultures knew without the science of today.

The biologist, Joan Borysenko has said "I can tell you as a biologist that when we step into the part of ourselves that doesn't judge, that is simply open to the possibilities of the moment, that what happens is we feel a sense of peace and gratitude. Enormous biochemical changes accompany that, changes in the neuropeptides from the emotional center of the brain, changes in our immune system and our cardiovascular system that are all consistent with good health."

In the difficult times that we live in it is more important than ever to "straighten up and fly right", as the old song goes. You might consider not even getting on the Titanic let alone changing seats.

CHANGING SEATS ON THE TITANIC

The brain is prepared to give us the circulation of certain chemicals....given to us by nature...to get out of our mess. Stop telling our stories over and over. It was my father or it was my sister or it was my mother or my husband or boss or, or, or that did this or that or whatever. No matter. It is up to US to take the responsibility for our story and to change the present so the future can change.

"Any intelligent fool can make things bigger and more complex... it takes a touch of genius... and a lot of courage to move in the opposite direction"

ALBERT EINSTEIN

THE SUBJECT OF RESISTANCE

This chapter was written, although in conjunction with me and consisting of all the different ideas I discussed over some time, by Marc Fischer, and so I begin and finish mostly in his words because, as I mentioned much earlier, I have no real idea of the resistance he bespeaks. I have, ofttimes, been quite skeptical and challenging, but not resistant.

Each Thursday afternoon, for the past few months, I've been meeting with a man who has been helping me write this book. An affable, forty-ish, graying short hair, glasses, button-down, short-sleeved oxford shirt-and-tie with trousers, Honda Odyssey and a laptop kind-of-guy. A married, with two young daughters, a little house in Westport, Connecticut, and a job in "operations" for a financial services firm in Westchester kind-of-guy. If not for his being a first-generation son of a pair of German artists (and an artist himself through he may not know it), he is the very model of New England conservatism. A heck of a nice man, with a quiet demeanor and a wry sense of humor, is this writer-man who visits my apartment, listening and recording and asking questions. He is (or was) as removed from this philosophy as a human being could be. In fact, when we first met (he would confide to me later), in the conference room a mutual friend and client who had the foresight to pair us up, and he listened to me discussing the substance and nature of the project we would be undertaking, he thought I was a "wing-nut".

We were talking one Thursday afternoon, this skeptic writer and I, about Emoto's book on water crystals called The Hidden Messages In Water, which was featured in the wonderful movie <u>What The Bleep Do We Know</u>.

Dr. Masaru Emoto discovered that crystals, formed in frozen water, reveal changes when specific, concentrated thoughts are directed toward them. Furthermore, he found that water crystals from clear springs and water, which have been exposed to loving words, shows brilliant, complex, and colorful snowflake patterns, while crystals from polluted water, or water exposed to negative thoughts, form incomplete, asymmetrical patterns with dull colors. Being nice to water makes it happy and content. Being mean and nasty to water makes it sad. The book is not merely a dry thesis, but is populated throughout with Dr. Emoto's stunning, evocative photography.

I began reading passages from the book to my guest. I read how Emoto believed that a direct relationship exists between negative and positive thoughts <u>and our own body chemistry</u>. What is each of us after all, but a sack of cells, each one comprised mainly of water? Emoto went on to relate that at the onset of the First Gulf War, as the first waves of bombs were going off in Iraq, he observed and recorded distinct changes occurring in water crystals in Japan, where he was doing his research. All this I related to my skeptic guest, who quietly jotted down his notes and nodded thoughtfully. When I was finished, I closed the book, and thrust it toward him.

"There...it's all there...in black and white...in color even!"

"It's true! He proves it in this book! Here...take it! Look! See! It's all right there!"

My blood was up. I get that way with skeptics, particularly the quiet ones. The ones who I know are smart, and who are turning the stuff around and round in their heads.

Then he said something I swear I've heard a thousand times before. He said: "These pictures are beautiful. It would be so nice to believe this stuff. I wish I could."

I sat back, smiled took a drink of water from my plastic bottle, and said: "Why can't you? What have you got to lose?"

You know what he answered? "My dignity. My self-respect. The respect of my peers."

So I told him this story.

I was sitting on my bed, watching TV one night. A movie was on. I can't remember which one; it may have even been just a regular old TV show like the Odd Couple. It doesn't matter. It's just not important to the story. The important part is, there was a camera shot of a busy Manhattan street, like 5th Avenue or Madison, right in mid-town, New York on a busy day, with the camera angle looking uptown. Literally thousands of people, a sea of people, walking on the sidewalks, and gridlock in the street. The scene was circa 1970's. You could tell by the way people were dressed, and by which model of taxis you could see.

The movie (or show) broke for commercial and as if by magic or some act of fate the commercial showed nearly the identical camera shot (busy Manhattan street, people, traffic), except this time it was 2005. Do you know what I saw (besides differently dressed people and newer taxis)?

Cell phones.

Fully 80 % of the people on the street, be they broker types in their Armani suits, or pretty secretaries, or Chinese food delivery guys, or the fellow selling ka-bobs from a push-cart had a cell phone pressed to his or her ear (except for the exceptionally cool ones with Bluetooth wireless ear pieces, who were taking advantage of even slicker double-wireless technology, and who *were looking every bit like lunatics...talking to themselves). Everyone was chatting away.*

If you would have told folks back in 1975 that in 30 years everyone would have a wireless phone, about the size of a Hershey bar, that took pictures and stored people's phone numbers inside, do you think they would have given you an ounce of respect? My God. you can't even find a pay phone in Manhattan today, at least not one that works! Back in 1974 you couldn't swing a dead cat in mid-town without hitting a bank of 5 or 6 pay-phones all lined up in a row (and all occupied for that matter)...with a line of 2 or 3 very annoyed looking people queued up, waiting to talk into the same filthy hand-set the person before them had been shouting into.

Yeah...your friends would have really respected you if you had laid that on them in 1975, Just like they would have respected you for letting them know that in only 25 years, they would be getting all of their information on everything from something called the **"Internet."**

Yup...people aren't going to buy those phones in a store! No sir! They're going to sign up for their wireless phone service and get the phone at a substantially reduced cost (or free with a 2 year subscription), by using their computer and doing something called "going online"!

Respect? Your 1975 friends would have been laughing so hard they'd have been blowing ooze out their nose.

Think about Edward Jenner and smallpox. In 1796 he acted upon the insane notion that milkmaids who contracted the cowpox disease never got smallpox. He extracted pus from the cowpox pustule on the hand of a milkmaid and inserted it into an incision on the arm of an 8-year-old boy. Think about how that one must have flown among the oh-so enlightened folk of the *late 18th century? Well...the boy contracted cowpox...but he never got smallpox! A disease that was responsible for the deaths of literally hundreds of millions of people was then and there going to be on the defensive, because Jenner asked: "What have I got to lose?", and he didn't answer "The respect of my peers?"*

Let's examine what we're talking about here through the enlightened, calculating eyes of our superior western sensibilities (stop laughing all you who are already onboard).

Human civilization is roughly 6,000 years old. The four oldest are the Mesopotamian, Egyptian, Indian and Chinese. In each of these civilizations, great emphases was and is still placed upon what I'll call spirituality. By spirituality, I'm referring to that which does not owe itself to daily existence. It was the realm of certain segments of the population to devote their entire lives to the study of spirituality, and over the course of thousands of years, as thousands of people whose sole purpose in life was to probe the mysteries of existence, plied their art, certain truths became self-evident (to borrow a phrase). Some of these are:

Sacred sound- There are sounds we humans can and do make, often (but not exclusively) during rites and rituals of a spiritual or mystic nature, which are not only conducive to a general feeling of corporal well-being, but which have the effect of allowing the participant to transcend their current state of consciousness. Sacred sounds cut across civilizations and are present in nearly all forms of spiritual and religious rites, and have their basis in simple vibration.

Meditation- A practiced art, whereby a person may reach an intensely contemplative state. Most often done, but not solely, with the use of a mantra. This continual use of letting everything "go" brings one to what is called in Quantum Physics as the Unified Field.

THE SUBJECT OF RESISTANCE

Yogic Flying- *This is discussed in a chapter by itself but is done through a combination of meditation and use of words or combination of words called sutras. The reason for learning such a thing is to create coherence both in the individual and the surrounding area, be it the home, the neighborhood or with enough people, the country or the world.*

Pulse Diagnosis- *a way of someone trained to do it, of listening to the pulses in one's wrist to tell what is happening in the body. In both India and China it was and is used as a diagnostic tool. There are not just a few pulses that can be felt, but many.*

The Forty Laws of Nature- *called in the Hindu world, the Vedas. You may have heard some of them recently popularized such as Ayurved under which would fall the practice of among other things, pulse diagnosis and more commonly known, Yoga and Pranayam (breathing techniques).*

Tai chi– and other martial arts came about at the same time as much of the knowledge of India. Besides what beauty one sees when observing the practice, it teaches the use of energy for both person health, and for fighting if necessary.

Shaman practices- One of these might be learning how to "lay" an altar in the ancient style of such countries as Peru and Guatemala. When on realizes how to do this, one would also realize the similarity between this and any other altar and practice at an altar.

What the mystics discovered, over the course of millennia, is that though meditation, and by invoking sacred sounds, a person can achieve many things. They can transcend their present state of consciousness, and achieve a feeling of unimaginable peace, tranquility and joy anytime, even during incredibly trying or stressful moments. They can find incalculable inner strength, which can be used to overcome *great pain or discomfort, or even to radiate and bestow strength, peace and tranquility to persons nearby who are not meditating. Persons trained in these arts can raise and lower body temperature at will, often to extreme levels. They can likewise, raise and lower heart rate and respiration. They can increase their capacity to learn. Through meditation and specialized training, a person can detect and cure illness and bring comfort to the afflicted. With the right knowledge, belief and training, a person can even use gravity in a way that they come off the ground in what we previously called Yogic Flying. Saint Theresa also did it in the church.*

All of these thing and more, are an integral part of the daily lives of countless millions of people who happen to live a few thousand miles away from us. Their beliefs and philosophies are thousands of years old, and are as "mainstream" in their countries as McDonald's and Tylenol are to us.

Journey to the Center of the Self

Why then would one resist?

People resist for 4 primary reasons:

Fear of failure

Fear of success

Fear of ridicule

Fear of change

Let's tackle the easiest one first, the fear of change. Most of us don't like change all that much. It represents risk and the unknown. Once we're outside of our comfort zone we're vulnerable and weak, so we avoid change wherever we can. But because most people who are reading this book are of a logical mind, I shouldn't take a great deal of effort to convince a person who is change-adverse to admit that without change there can be little progress. Moreover, I'm not advocating a sea change here. No one is asking you to move your family to India and join an ashram. I'm not suggesting you should take a month's leave of absence from your job so you can travel to Iowa and take courses at the Maharishi University (although I know that Max probably would). I am suggesting that you open your mind to the notion that these concepts and philosophies are good and true, and should not be dismissed.

Fear of failure is a biggie. Some have it worse than others. I know some who don't seem to have any fear of failure at all, and I'm always envious. But there's no real "failure" here to worry about. There's no test and no grade point average. The only failure I can see would be if someone got so bound up that they could, under no circumstances, let some of these thoughts into their life...and that would be more of a "loss" anyway...wouldn't it?

I'll see if I can help by starting off with this little secret: Here in America...we're a little up tight. Yes....here in the good old USA we've got more issues than God made little green apples. We've got problems with black people, and Muslims, homosexuals and the obese; we've got problems with Democrats and Republicans, artsy people, vegetarians and people who drink beer when they're 18 years old. Most people find their cliques pretty early on in life, and darned if they don't live those entire lives not too-too far outside of that clique (Max calls it crystallizing).

My friend, the writer, actually said that he was worried what some of the parents at his daughter's day care would think about him and his family if they found out he actually believed in this stuff. Do you know what I told him?

"Who cares!?"

"Who cares what you believe in? Really and truly...who cares?"

"No one is asking you to bring a box and stand on it in the middle of downtown Westport, Connecticut and start preaching through a bullhorn about the benefits of eastern philosophy and Reiki to the stay-at-home moms and their au pairs hustling to the Lilly Pulitzer sale."

"No one is going to ridicule you, or your wife, or your little girls, because you accept a philosophy based on truth, simplicity and love, which happens to have it's roots in India...because no one is going to know!"

"Of course, if you happen to be at a Greenwich cocktail party, and the wife of the CEO of a Fortune 500 company and you get talking, while snacking on cracked crab, and she happens to mention that she and her husband have begun a regimen of meditation and Reiki consultations as a stress-management therapy, because their friend's daughter was exposed to it (with marvelous results, she might add) when she was a patient at the Maria Ferrari Children's Hospital...well then...won't you look smart when you mention that you helped to write a chapter in this book."

That last one stopped him in his tracks. He sat back, took off his little wire-rimmed glasses, lowered his head, shut and pinched the corners of his eyes with his thumb and forefinger, and with eyes still closed, just started chuckling softly through his nose and shaking his head.

"You're right." He said. "no one would really ever know....and even if they did...who the hell would really care...and even if they did really care...what the hell would I really care about that."

"Exactly." I said.

The fear of success isn't exactly one of those fears I feel too sorry about. You see, I have some friends who are perennial underachievers. Bright, creative, lovely people who somewhere along the line got it into their noggins that things are always better exactly as they are (and that the alternatives are actually a hell of a lot worse). There's my friend who has three teaching degrees, but who never stops going to school never accepts a teaching post because he's always horrified by the politics involved in the profession. I have another friend who used to write guidance system computer code for the navy, and whose hobbies include game and string theory, but who is currently driving a zamboni at a Colorado ice skating rink because he can't handle the "pressures" of his former job. Let's put it this way. If you are not going to open your mind to what we have been talking about because you think you are going to be too successful, well, what can we say? Can we say that you are concerned about becoming the world's best mediator or the next incarnation of the Dalai Lama? If you fear that you maybe one of only a handful of people whom in the last 6,000 some odd years has achieved total consciousness or enlightenment, I can't help you.

"We usually don't look. We overlook"
ALAN WATTS

"If you reject the food, ignore the customs, fear the religion and avoid the people, better stay home"

ANONYMOUS

THE EXPERIENCE OF FLYING...
WITHOUT A PLANE
(OR WHAT DOES IT REALLY MEAN TO SURRENDER?)

Well, where to begin this journey.....and it was a journey overdue. After taking the course in 1972 in Transcendental Meditation (TM) with Maharishi Mahesh Yogi, yes, the Yogi of the Beatles, and receiving my personal mantra, I moved on with other things. For some 35 years I have never not practiced my TM. What I have explained in another chapter about how I was challenged by Jiri Sipijlo and by my never-ending need to experience before I could have an opinion, I was initiated in TM.

Journey to the Center of the Self

In those days there were lines of people at a New York hotel and it seemed everyone was getting initiated. Not a bad idea, really. This was a special sacred experience given only by your Guru (if you could find one, he or she was really good, and most importantly would accept you as a Chela, student). At least the energy was going to change in a big way and the world would be altered even if it never realized. These were the days of the "Flower Children" and I was on the fringe.

Happily, my day of expression in dress, idea and modified lifestyle were more prevalent. Not so much amongst my friends but around. Women were not allowed to wear trousers, particularly not in restaurants and "decent" places. I wore a white silk Nehru pantsuit with white designer boots into the airport and onto a Pan Am plane headed for Paris. Was I just not it? My husband thought it was no big deal; he never thought anything was a big deal. He got on the plane, asked me where we were going and fell asleep. How charming and romantic, sharing this great adventure with your wife and falling asleep. Champagne and caviar were my favorite first class items so for a little while I was content. Not for long.

It was night and because I was wearing pants, when I saw the Captain he asked me if I wanted to fly into Paris in the cockpit. Oh my, those were the days. OK, lest I not digress too far, the experience of TM must continue. Please read on.

I had an experience that was not much different than what I was currently using as a mantra. As a mater of fact, my mantra and technique worked way faster and deeper than this one. I decided to give it a chance for four months. After that time I was experiencing a similar state of consciousness. Connection with the Unified Field is how a Quantum Physicist would explain it. It was a feeling unexplainable but so lovely and sweet that I felt constantly rejuvenated.

Journey to the Center of the Self

It was a place that I always procrastinated going to but once on the trip I was blissful. What I mean to say is that even today, some thirty odd years later, I still procrastinate sitting down to begin my mantra. Once I settle in and begin it is still very relaxing at the least. I am now able to experience the silence. The true silence, even in the midst of a loud airport or room. This is the amazing thing. I feel that I can be in the middle of life and yet be able to be clear, centered and aware. I feel I am an observer at the same time a participant. Knowing that I am participating in an illusion not unlike watching a movie and yet being an actor in that movie. **SURRENDER IS A HUGE PART OF THIS WHOLE EXPERIENCE**, which I never had even a hint of in the beginning. Understanding **surrender**, as I have said, is critical. Consider **surrender** a process of excavation. As contractors need to clear, grade and excavate an area <u>before</u> they even begin to pour a foundation, the concept of

surrender must precede the steps that follow.

Here's how it works:

I spoke before about a "perceived unavailable parent"....we each have (or had) the perception of a parent who was in one way or another emotionally unavailable. I should be very clear here...the word "perception" is important. The parent of whom I speak may be anything but emotionally unavailable...the key is ...to us, they were missing. This then, began to shape our response to life. "Daddy's not there for me...so am I going to become an introvert, a wall-flower, a rebel, an artist, a comedian, a concert pianist, a doctor, a lawyer or a drunk."

The perceptions of our parents, which we develop, early in life, form the essence of ourselves (no epiphany here). In order for us to truly accept new thoughts, ideas, emotions and concepts (especially the incredibly complex concepts we will be discussing), we need to identify the source of those perceptions (the things that created the essence of ourselves)...<u>and let them go.</u>

Let me put it another way, drill down a little further: We are the product of a great many things, strands of DNA, molecules, electrons, sub-atomic particles, cells, proteins, water, our parents, our surroundings...all of these things make up what we are. But the essence, our essence, is the perceptions we carry of our parents.

If we can teach ourselves to let those perceptions go, to accept, to **surrender,** we can effectively wipe out a lifetime of useless baggage. Baggage that will continually conspire to prejudice our thoughts, befuddle our senses and create walls of doubt and suspicion. An example I use to illustrate: A friend and I were talking (really he was talking...unburdening himself really...great grey cumulus clouds of depressing downer talk), "my life sucks...it's such a drag...blah, blah, blah."

I shouted at him: "Transcend! Rise above!" He looked at me as though I had 3 heads and a beak. He did not speak the same language. Through my life's work, my training and my study, I learned to **surrender**. I have few preconceptions, no prejudice, and little baggage. I have not "crystallized" (nor do I intend to anytime soon.) My mind remains open, at all cost, to new thoughts, ideas, emotions and concepts. It is a club my despondent friend cannot yet join.

As I write this chapter, I realize that at 65 years of age, I've spent the better part of 50 years in this process I call **surrender**. The lessons of that sentence are two fold. First; never give up, and second; you don't need to <u>completely</u> surrender to begin this process, you need to understand and embrace the concept.

YOGIC FLYING. There...that got your attention. Please don't moan, groan or close your mind to what I'm about to describe. Remember...s-u-r-r-e-n-d-e-r. Do not preconceive or prejudge. Do not crystallize.

When I was young, about 8 or 10 years old, I believed I could fly. I so believed this, that one afternoon, I gathered about twenty of my Stamford, CT neighborhood friends together and announced to all that I was going to fly...right down Sagamore Road (I even fashioned a cape and tied it around my neck.) With all the neighborhood kids watching and with full confidence that I could do this, I ran, full tilt down the hill, screamed "shazam!" as my favorite comic character did and leaped into the air.

Nothing. I mean NOTHING. I was devastated when I fell on my rear end. The crowd dispersed and I shuffled home, despondent and confused. My mother laughed and I cried.

My mother did not exactly ridicule me but it felt like that. She wanted to show me that I was silly for thinking I could defy gravity, but it didn't take me long to return to my belief that I could do anything. I would try to fly in many ways before I found my true calling and every one of those experiences would help me to learn to recognize my power. **THINK ABOUT THIS IN TERMS OF YOUR OWN LIFE**.

So, many years after my attempt to "fly" down the street with all my friends watching I, now at 52 or 53, signed up to take a yogic flying course. I even got three of my students to join me. Please understand, at 53 I was no novice. I was already a Reiki Master. I had studied breathing techniques and yoga and mantra chanting. I had studied past life regression, iridology, astrology, most philosophies and most religions. I had availed myself of thousands of books and workshops (some quite enlightening and some major rip-offs); you have read my account of my most diverse life.

Journey to the Center of the Self

The summer of the experience with my Croatian friends, mentioned in my chapter on In Search of the Miraculous, was probably the most extraordinary time in my life. What I had known about for over 18 years and put off as unscientific and impossible, I was seeing in front of my own eyes and experiencing the energy at a level previously unheard of. So in some way, because of my "prove it" mind, I had missed 18 years of flying. Perhaps that was as it was supposed to be, but now seeing believed, and I believed.

Ivan assured me that I could do the flying even though Ivan Kulac failed to actually lift off when he took the course. This only means that he did not leave the ground, but not that the energy was not had, nor that some of the blocks were not removed. Coherence was experienced anyway but most probably in a different way.

In the fall of 1993 I reunited with TM and found a circle of people who

taught TM and were also long time flyers.
One must have two teachers recommend
you and you must attend at least one
weekend residential course. It must be
clear that you can maintain yourself in
the middle of many people meditating
with you throughout the weekend. Of
course after the time with Ivan and most
probably way before, I had no problems
at all. I found the whole thing quite
amusing. What I did encounter,
however, was a book of Dr. Deepak
Chopra called Perfect Health. This book
changed my life in a more subtle way. It
was not my introduction to Ayurvedic
eating and living because I had already
lived a summer of that with the
Croatians. What it did was deeply
explain the principals of this kind of
living to me and the idea of living by the
laws of Nature. When you live by the
laws of Nature, Nature seems to support
you. Thus I changed the way I ate, the
time of sleep and arising, I learned about
music of the Universe called Gandharva
Veda which was at varying times

enlivening and at times relaxing. I learned that if the vibrations played in the home even when no one was at home it had an effect on the living environment. It was a time of paradigm shift in my consciousness and therefore my way of life, both in thinking and living.

The other great gift was meeting a TM teacher, Kathy Connors. She was contrary to so much of what I was and knew. I liked her instantly because I recognized that although we thought differently, she apparently lived what she preached. A rare thing for me to find. Over time we became friends and it was she and another gentleman who I had met that sponsored me in the Yogic Flying Course, or CIC.

The reviewing process was neither short nor easy but I began in New Haven, Connecticut over a few weekends to study the necessary components to later go to Fairfield, Iowa to complete my course.

I had for some time had a meditation group of some eight or twelve people who got together at my house on Sundays. One of Bakic's clients went with me to the weekends and when we meditated with the Sunday group there was a noticeable change in energy. All participants recognized it and my long time friend and my roommate decided to join the next course. We waited some months (the course in Iowa was only given twice a year).

I had long heard of the masters of yoga who purportedly "flew". As did, they say, Saint Catherine. I had read books on the subject and had asked many teachers and friends about the practice. It was inconceivable that I not explore this. The course was in Fairfield, Iowa at the Maharishi International University, which meant taking a flight from JFK to Chicago, then catching a connecting flight to Grand Rapids. United Airlines lost my luggage, a first for me after a lifetime of travel. Oh well, probably sold at the store in Georgia.

There were roughly 56 women and probably an equal amount of men, all flying in to take the course with me (men and women do not take the course together, they are segregated, and most probably with good cause). My fellow, aspiring yogic flyers (all 100 or so of them) are, for the most part, extremely well educated and worldly people. Not the "granola" type one might be thinking. Most are fairly well off. I bring it up only to paint a picture.

The airline lost my luggage....permanently, and to compensate....they bought me a couple of jumper-type sweats. I should add that the course requires full banquet attire for the evening meal so I had brought all of my best clothes. The clothes were pieces that I had purchased over the years in many different countries. "What was the lesson?" I asked myself. I was not attached to material goods, so why? The only benefit in the end was I had two jumper suits, one pair of warm boots a Chinese hat and an ankle length coat from Indonesia. At least I had those. Most importantly I was the only really comfortable one all the time. In a room full of well-dressed meditation students, I was the only one wearing an orange jumper. It was pretty funny.

Anyway....it was a 2-week course. Without divulging things I am not supposed to divulge, here's what happened. During the 2 weeks, each day, each student would spend a significant portion of the day alone, in meditation.

In our rooms, we would meditate, recite our mantra, perform our breathing and yoga asanas, and go through our list of learned ancient knowledge. Each of these complete sessions would last between 30 minutes and an hour and a half. Afterward we would rest and then repeat the process, exactly as before. Over and over. A break for lunch, a group meeting and discussion to break the routine and clear the mind; some special music was played that kept us in sync with the vibration of the universe, but after that, back we would go, yoga, breath, meditation, special instructions and so on and so on. Each time, spiritually (and physically) approaching and attaining consecutively higher and higher planes of consciousness. Somewhere in the middle of the course, we were ready, we were ripe, and our instructors gave us the last and final instruction. With this, our group would now have the final piece of the puzzle by which we could now do something none of us had EVER done before.

I should digress, as you see I often have a want to do, because I know some readers may at this point be skeptics. Prior to my signing up for the course, and after 18 years of knowing about and laughing at the course, I had personally witnessed a yogic flyer perform this amazing process. My Reiki Master from Croatia, Ivan Bakic came to the US to stay in my house in 1993 for what was supposed to be one month but turned out to be nearly six the first year and five the second year.

Each morning, when we woke and showered, we would begin the day with the same routine. At 6:00a.m. each morning, we would begin chanting sacred sound, mantras, breathing, and meditation and then he would **FLY**. He was, I later learned, not suppose to fly in front of me and further more not with me if I was a woman and not married to him. I explained earlier, that I carry no prejudice, have little baggage, had begun working on **surrendering**, and accept most of what I see, but this was simply incredible. This slightly built man began and ended each day by doing something so wonderful, so mysterious, so seemingly impossible and so beautiful, as to defy all reason...and the feeling in the room after, well, I have no words to describe.

Then, he would push his mat to the side have a big laugh with me and we would go about the work of the rest of our day, he carrying with him an inner peace and strength that can only be described as invincibility.

I WANTED invincibility and more than that I wanted to create coherence for the world and myself.

So now, in Fairfield, Iowa, in a meeting hall, joined by 56 like-minded (maybe) women and several pairs of instructors, having practiced and worked for a week, I was about to receive the last piece of the puzzle, the key to the invincibility I had borne witness to. One of my friends and I had, of course, tried, in a cross legged position to perform the act of raising off the ground. We could indeed, with great effort, move up slightly but with great difficulty and a lot of perspiration. What did we know? We had to at least try. Once again, here I was, so excited to receive the knowledge of invincibility. One of the instructors spoke the last special instruction, everyone began their mantras....the instructor rang a bell....and I couldn't remember what she had said.

I didn't just forget it...it didn't register. I asked the instructor to repeat. She did...and I lost it again....a very, very simple instruction, indeed. Repeat, lost. Repeat, lost. It was becoming a joke.

My friend and I had been separated for joking and laughing too much and here I was with something really laughable. This couldn't be happening. I closed my eyes and began my process from the beginning. When the instructor rang the bell again and it was time to inwardly repeat the special instruction (that I had forgotten), I must have surrendered because I told myself "This is it, this is the end of your 2 weeks. You've had a wonderful time. Met some terrific people. You learned a great deal about yourself. You've attained a higher level of consciousness and understanding than you have ever reached before...just enjoy....just accept...who cares if you fly or not...detach yourself from the outcome...take joy in the doing and the outcome takes care of itself...It doesn't matter if you fly or not." And in that moment, that very moment, IT HAPPENED. I really flew...lift off...what is more I was the first to pop. Soon two others joined me. I fell over in the most rapturous of joy I have ever experienced. I felt gratitude to the whole world, the whole universe, I wanted to laugh uncontrollably but the room was silent.

Slowly, each day more and more of the group "took off". You can only imagine the power. It was indescribable. There was the tremendous joy and the tremendous gratitude. I really felt INVINCIBLE and HUNGRY. I felt hungry as never before and that made me want to laugh again. When you can wake up each morning, move over to your flying mat, go through your routine (granted a rather sophisticated one)...and fly, literally hop up into the air with great ease and grace, you don't just feel invincible, you ARE invincible.

Following the experience of Yogic Flying we were exposed to the playing of the recitations of the Rig Veda because the sound from this creates in us a specific physiology, behavior and mode of functioning which induces the direct experience of the Sacred. It affects the nervous system directly. Think how much sound we are exposed to daily and how we think so little of how it affects our entire physiology.

Think how color and sound are both vibrations and this was well known by Pythagoras (remember from school when you studied about the isosceles triangle?) To refresh your memory it went like this "The square of the hypotenuse of any right triangle is equal to the sum of the square or the other two sides." This was Pythagoras. I will go no further because then we begin a discussion of stringed instruments, etc. which were also addressed by Pythagoras way before any of us were born.

I have been "flying" now for twelve years and I continue to be amazed. I am picking up the ending of this chapter and it is now a Sunday afternoon in August of 2006. The war between Israel and Hezbollah is raging and in many places in the world, including here in the United States in Washington, D.C. and in Fairfield, Iowa, hundreds of "Yogic Flyers" are flying for coherence. The fly is for creating peace in the world and at the moment to relieve the stress in the Middle East.

How can that be done, you might be asking yourself. She is definitely off the mark, a few stories short of an office building. I am not. If you have seen the movie What the Bleep do we Know you will remember a Dr. John Hagelin who was bespeaking the results of a study done in D.C. in the summer of 1993. At that time, 4,000 Yogic Flyers were gathered for a Peace Assembly. They were flying for hours of the day and the results after six weeks was that the crime rate in the middle of the hot summer was reduced by approximately 28%. When they left the crime rate slowly increased.

For those of you, who study yoga as more than just an exercise, think about this. I am sure you have heard of Patanjali, the author of the Yoga-Sutra (circa 100BCE.) It is on his principles and his sutras that we are able to fly. Think also how long ago this knowledge was known and available and how long it has taken those of us who "fly" to believe and participate.

My friend Winnie and I are planning to go to D.C. in a week or two to join in the flying to make America Invincible. Strange perhaps, but when you understand the basic physics you don't think so. Better to sit together with the ability to create peace than to get out the guns.

It is my understanding that at this time the only country that bought into Maharishi's idea is Mozambique. This country trained a percentage of their army to do the flying and although they had their share of floods and other natural disasters, THE FIGHTING IN THAT AREA QUIETED. If there is anything here that you find you are unable to believe why not look up all the research. I still, from time to time, resist the going to sit down and begin my program but once begun it creates a long-term difference both for my neighborhood and myself.

SURRENDER to the possibility!

Friend from Africa with Max
- first two flyers

"What the eye sees is extra"
ARABIC SAYING

"Imagination is more important than knowledge"

SIGN HANGING IN EINSTEIN'S PRINCETON OFFICE

THE I-CHING ON THE CAKE

The I-Ching is an ancient form of "seeing your future" or your way to proceed, a Chinese method of using coins or sticks to throw and interpreting their meaning. In some way I want to speak in this chapter about the process I used to amend with my mother. Most probably it was the way that the Universe gave me as a choice if I wanted to follow it and clean what was, most likely, a very large Karma. I use the phrase I-Ching instead of saying this just "put the icing on the cake" for the story that follows.

In 2001 my mother called me and said that the family member who she had been living with for some years, although independently, was not prepared to take her with them when retirement and/or moving occurred. They were also not willing to take care of her when it was no longer appropriate for her to live with any increased assistance. Caretaking was not part of the package. She never realized this and expected to be forever in what she considered her home.

Speaking only for myself, and my belief, I think that the "parent ships" bring us into life and it is our responsibility to help them, when the time comes, in their process of leaving. Some families think that nursing or assisted living facilities are more appropriate for them. I suppose each family has a reason for their decisions.

In 2001 in the late evening, I received a call from my mother. She was very disturbed and did not know what to do with the information that had been given to her. Her question was should she consider moving to a "home" or did I have another suggestion. Although I was not my mother's favorite child nor was she the parent that I related to the most (for me she was my perceived unavailable parent), I immediately told her to move in with me, and that I would care for her as needed. She was greatly relieved and said she had hoped I would ask her. I immediately followed this conversation with a call to the person she lived with and asked if my mother was correct in her understanding of what had been said to her....it seemed so far fetched to me because I had asked my mother to come and live with me at the time she wanted to move originally. She had made friends, went to the health club, played bridge, did her own shopping, etc. and many times took evening meals with the family. To my complete dismay, I was assured that the conversation was correct.

With this background in mind, I considered what I had agreed to and why. My mother was the person in my life who always seemed to have little faith in my lifestyle, my hopes and wishes, my creativity, and particularly in my desire to help others in a "hands on way". She felt that I had way too much energy from the get-go and being the business, money-conscious woman that she was, I was a disaster waiting to happen. Working on the street with homeless kids in this county and others was not her idea of what I should be doing. Married to an acceptable professional and going to the country club was more of what she had in mind.

I looked at this as an opportunity to clean the differences, or Karma, if you will, between us. If people love and respect each other they can, I believe, work out a mutually satisfying relationship together. I did not know exactly how I felt about her nor did I know how she really felt about me (perhaps as a good bet for caretaking) but for sure I felt it was my responsibility and opportunity to try and make a lifetime, not so good situation, into a great one.

A few months later my mother moved into my house. I sold some of my furniture and made room for her belongings in an attempt to soften the blow of changing everything she knew and felt comfortable with at the age of 88.

She wanted to stay in my room rather than the one put aside for her because she said it made her feel safe and cozy. For me this was not a problem, as privacy with those close to me was not an issue. I could understand how she must have felt being suddenly uprooted from the familiar life she had become accustomed to.

For the first few months both of us had a real adjustment. She was somewhat, as she said, disoriented to the idea of starting again with new people and places and happenings. She had not brought with her any of her medical, dental, or legal files and so my work life came to a halt until I could find her the right doctors, dentist, and lawyer and figure out how to arrange for all these records to be assembled and sent.

Change of insurance, mail address, social security checks, change of state driver's license, auto registration, auto insurance, the all-important hairdresser and in general a huge amount of labor intensive work to get her basic life in order.

I was now responsible for on-time meals twice a day and getting her out and about so she could begin her bridge games, helping her to set up her bank accounts and meet the new professional people she would need as fast as possible. I felt as overwhelmed as she did until we could both get our lives in a new pattern. It took a while but she began to drive (after consuming a sizable amount of chocolate cake, which she always loved. I never realized the power of chocolate) and I went to the local senior center and library (she always adored reading and the Greenwich library) so that she would not have to find her way alone in the beginning. After that she was on a roll and after the second year or so found a boyfriend. This is a funny story all to itself, but I shall choose to keep her secrets private.

It took some time on my part to keep my Reiki practice going during this period because planning my personal life was near impossible. I took her, with much pleasure, everywhere I went, thinking that new stimulation would help her feel part of my little family. My son lived nearby and came relatively often with his girlfriend de jour, to visit. This made her happy because they would always take her to her favorite discount clothing store where she had been going for many years. For my part, because I had to get her to go to the senior center I promised to go each week with her. This was, for me, a bit of torture, to put it mildly, but in the process I did learn to play Mah-Jong.

In an effort to get to the real point here I shall say that for the first year or so we had our battles. She was a great actress as well as a person adept at putting aside those things she chose not to deal with and things that could easily "push my buttons". Without a moment of hesitation I can say that once she felt settled we began to play out our old familiar parts with each other. We provoked each other and challenged each other until finally I could really see the entire picture of our cycle both from her side and mine.

I was no easier to deal with for her than she was for me. These patterns were exactly what I was looking for even though they never felt too good for either of us. I began to come to understandings and to clearly see what had happened all our lives. We began, even though in the beginning she resisted, to discuss our feelings and thoughts openly. She slowly came to see me as I was and not as she wanted to see me, and the same happened with me. We worked hard at understanding and accepting.

Because she was always nearby when I saw my patients and she heard all of my conversations with friends as well as those I had with business possibilities, she came to recognize and respect me (she used to say "where did you learn all of these things? And we laughed about that often) and I came to feel extremely loving and respectful of her feelings of worry and vulnerability. Slowly we were making progress. For my part I was losing all my childhood anger and hurt toward her and for her part she would say, "I never realized that you were so much like my mother" and "you are the only one since my parents that ever did so much for me". In the beginning I was sure she was manipulating me with these words to curry my favor and assure herself of her safety but as time went on and we became closer I realized she meant what she said and I could hear her without my old "child ears".

In many ways I was now acting as, her mother, and this gave me the opportunity to work hard, slowly by slowly, to avoid replicating the behavior I had felt she used with me when I was a child. I was exhilarated by these day-to-day discoveries. They gave me continual pleasure because I knew that I was giving up all the old feelings and responses (perhaps not as fast as I would have liked, but surrendering them all the same.) I began to feel the internal and intellectual sense of surrender. Each in our own way we came to love and appreciate each other for who we were. Most importantly she came to trust me in my decision-making.

We spoke often of the need to finish our journey with each other before she made her final journey. We talked about forgiveness not only with each other, but also with the people she was still unhappy with but would not confront. My mother was never one who wanted to directly confront or be put in a bad light.

These traits, I realized, were family and societal trainings of her time, as they existed in her sisters as well. She said during these conversations that she wanted to, but direct expression of her real feelings was very difficult. As time went by she wanted to write and be clear about things. I think she felt it was easier than having to speak directly and make a potential argument. These events were not well taken by those she told her true feelings to but she felt better when she did and I felt better because I did not have to make explanations for her (putting me in a precarious position.)

Somewhere during this time of forgiveness and explanation I remember trying to do the same with my sister, mostly because I saw her resembling my mother while I thought and acted more like my father and I felt it was necessary that we make decisions for our aging mother together. In this light, I must have been about 65 years old making her around 60. I asked her if we could not find a way to communicate so we would not misunderstand each other. We always had, but I felt we were of an age and understanding of life that we could at least attempt a try. I remember the deep emotional dismay and disappointment when she said, "No way, it can never happen."

But once again, I digress. My point in all of this is to share with you my most important finding about family matters which I find seep into all of our relationships in one way or another. Because I have had my share of tumultuous relationships and encounters and being a person of close self-examination most of my life, I have become somewhat of a self-appointed guru of such matters.

I have always been a very sensitive person although perhaps not always appearing so on the outside. I wanted family more than anything. I just loved the traditional idea of it with the emphasis on idea or better "ideal" of it where you have a group of people who want to support and help each other in their individual pursuits in life and also to be there for love and "wound licking" as it were.

Not having it definitely taught me how to give and become it for others and myself. The ultimate family member is the Divine. I grew in this idea and formed my own little personally made up family and as I early on divorced but for many years kept a very close relationship with my ex-husband (it took 14 years to go from separation to divorce because neither my husband nor my son wanted divorce and it really did not matter to me.) I was able to do this because as I saw it this way....when you leave your high school teacher to go onto college you are not angry at you high school teacher....and so it is, I think, with relationships of this nature.

I have never disliked my ex-husband or any other people that are part of my past because they were all, in their way, teachers for me and hopefully me for them. In the last eight or ten years I have slowly developed a way of loving (not necessarily liking) those with whom I cannot work out differences or who, for their own reasons and/or Karma, betray, resent, are jealous of, lie to me or to themselves, et. al. In my way I wish them the very best in their way through life but must lovingly, detach from them. In some way they become part of my past and I do not make a habit of going back to it because the lesson has already been learned. No sense trying to make something happen that does not appear to want to happen.

Most people feel compelled to hang onto almost everything. I say, divorce yourself from everything negative if you have learned all you can. You cannot make someone love you and you most probably cannot change his or her thinking. After all, it is quite a job just to change your own thinking. Again, love and respect are the only necessary ingredients for any relationship to prosper. It does not hurt to have a bit more than a pinch of compassion either, does it?

Look at your pattern, do the energy work to release the old junk from your cells and mind and surrender to whatever you consider the Divine.

In November of 2003, my mother began to have nosebleeds. I found myself taking her to the hospital every few days and one day the doctor called and said he had consulted with the ENT doctor and they had decided to take her off of her daily baby aspirin. I never thought about it because I thought she was covered with her coumadin (blood thinner for her artificial heart valve) as far as forming clots that would cause her a stroke. It kept my close friend Winnie (my mother considered her another grandchild) and I quite nervous and so we stayed close, never leaving her out of sight.

About four days after the removal of the aspirin and on a day that I was making the final preparations for Thanksgiving, I walked around the corner for a moment and only a moment, only to see my mother starting to have what appeared to me (I worked in neurology and neurosurgery for some years) to be a stroke. The left side of her mouth was starting to drop and she was talking but not making sense. I immediately took her hands and pushed my healing energy into her and kept talking and made her keep talking. I, of course, had pushed her "life-line" button and the ambulance was on its way. I must tell you I could, as wordy as I am, not express the extreme feeling that was pouring through my body while I kept pushing energy and reassuring her. I wanted to scream or pass out, etc. but had to be calm and decisive. As the emergency personnel got her ready for the ambulance I called my son and on the way to the hospital I called Winnie (on her way to Long Island, N.Y. to her family for the holiday) and told her to start distance Reiki healing but not to come back.

I drove behind the ambulance as to have a way of returning home after. I cried and prayed the whole way. I was sending light and Winnie was sending Reiki.

Arriving at the emergency room I went into action. Inside I felt, at first, as though I was coming undone but I had to be alert to everything to really be of service to my mother. She, on the other hand, was worried that if she could not speak correctly, how would she bid in her bridge games. While I worked for over four hours to push energy through her feet I kept her speaking and laughing and bidding her bridge plays. Meanwhile, I dealt with the doctors and other personnel who were amazed at how fast she was suddenly recovering. She had definitely had a severe stoke, so said the MRI, etc. but she was immediately beginning to show less and less symptoms.

My son read the newspaper and occasionally spoke to his grandmother, assuring her that everything would be fine.

It took many hours but finally we had her comfortably situated in a room and after a while we went home. It was the end of a very long day for all of us.

After a week of watching my mother, her tests, and her medications, I finally took her home. Almost as good as new, but still requiring an immense amount of care. I brought in a physical therapist and a speech therapist to assist in the few deficits remaining. Slowly I got her walking her usual one half hour per day and doing her mouth and hand exercises. Winnie and I worked each day with Reiki and when I took her for her check-up with the neurologist he was amazed at how well she maintained her balance and how little deficit she had considering the major amount of brain damage that she had incurred. He asked what I did and how amazing it was that she had resolved so quickly almost back to normal.

This was the last scare for what seemed like many years. I still had to push like a human tape recorder. Drink your water. Eat more protein. Have some fruit....take your walk. It was unending but it paid off. By doing this routine and keeping her blood levels accurately (she was, as I mentioned before on a blood thinner for her artificial heart valve) she really continued to thrive.

We had, through this experience, become closer than ever. We were the only ones who had gone through this experience and come out on top. She was back to wanting chocolate and that was the telltale sign.

Life continued along a relatively smooth course with the exception of family disruptions. I expect this is normal in every family and I was no longer surprised at the apparent lack of support for her by other members of her family. We continued our life. Went to movies and other outings together, she, Winnie, Winnie's dog (which we all considered a family member) and me. We were our own little family of four. Ok, we could not take Lettuce, the dog, to New York for the weekend to see The Lion King (my mother's great desire since its opening) or to the little evening soirées at the Plaza and Chez Josephine, but we had him at each birthday for, what else, chocolate mousse cake. He would sit on the floor while we ate and my mother talked with him.

I use these loving scenes as a backdrop to the coming events.

In late 2005 I was lying in bed in my room and I heard a loud thump. I ran to my mother's room only to find her in her bathroom, blood on the walls and everywhere else, and she on the floor and frightened....I was horrified and terrified. I am not sure which prevailed. It was ten at night and she had no idea what had happened. I checked her until I found the skin tear on her arm and attended to the wound and got her into bed.

This, I suppose you could say, was the beginning of the end. The doctor (Dr. Slogoff, who I had come to really trust) told me that she would continually get worse and that I should call Hospice. I was in complete shock. Six months to a year? She seemed so vital in spirit and yet frail in body. Her ability to concentrate and her short-term memory was lessening. Much of the time we could laugh and live as usual but she could not be left alone for any amount of time. I could not risk her falling again. But just as the doctor had said (he was always correct in his assessment but a little early in his timing), she fell many times and needed constant care. I moved her, once again, into my room where I could watch that she did not get out of bed at night.

I arranged for Hospice and eventually more help so I could food shop and carry on the daily chores. Many times I continued to take her with me. She HAD to go to the hairdresser (her friend Gary who was always so loving and kind to her) and of course, have her nails done. I had hired, some months ago, a lovely woman from Brazil, Adriana Silva. My mother related and was most comforted by her patience and deep, quiet caring and I was grateful to have such a fine person to help me.

As time went on I signed my mother up for a once a week adult day care where she could be more stimulated and have more people her own age to relate to. Her walking was becoming difficult because of an infected skin tear on her leg. She needed complete help in bathing and dressing. Although she continued to glance at her beloved New Yorker magazine and skim through books, her focus was failing. She hated the sides I had to add to the bed so she would not get up alone to go to the bathroom. I felt so sorry and would tell her stories so she could go peacefully to sleep and try and ignore or forget the bed rails. Between Adriana and I, we would finally get her to sleep.

This was a sad and VERY labor-intensive time for us all. Daily nurse visits, twice-weekly physical therapy with her super smart "pal" Lori Barger, walking with her everywhere she went all of the time.

On or around March 15th of 2006 she came home so very tired from her day at what we had come to call "senior camp". I spoke to the director of the care group and she sent me a photo of my mother that was wonderful. She had planted a plant in a small container, had a huge, happy smile on her face, her red leather jacket setting off the whiteness of her newly coiffed hair and all looked well. It was not well at all for after this day she never came upstairs again. She was 93, had an infection on her leg, was extremely fatigued and just wanted to stay in bed.

The decline was faster than I could keep up with. Before long I was getting no more than 2 or 3 hours of sleep a night...not enough for me under normal circumstances. I hired a nurse for the late night shift. The daily nervousness of constant decision-making was exhausting. I felt so sorry for her but always tried to preserve her dignity, as did the nurses. With difficulty we would move her to a chair to keep her moving. Her physical therapist, Lori Barger, would keep her range of motion as much as possible. Without her my mother would have had very little change or much movement, and getting from bed to chair would have been almost impossible. Adriana became quite adept at moving her but Winnie and I were just a disaster, not so much at getting her to the chair but to the little movable toilet. I must say in the middle of all this we had our moments of great humor. We were so inept but so determined.

With all of this and more, one day her breathing became very labored. I called the on duty Hospice nurse and we decided with the doctor to give her oxygen. She was allergic to the antibiotic she was taking and so on and so forth. I had promised her and myself to keep her home and let her pass from here with me.

She already had a hospital bed and now oxygen. My sleep was not what you would call peaceful.

On the days she would want me to crawl into bed with her I knew she was feeling better but those days, until the very end, were few and far between. I made special food for her. For a while she would only let me feed her until she finally let her favorite, Adriana, feed her as well. Adriana was a goddess sent for me and my mother. Calm and patient and kind, my mother liked her so much. Of course I must mention her nurse Pat from Hospice because not only was she proficient in her skills but also very patient and kind. I would, most often, laugh at what I called her "Revolutionary War" bandages and said that she was trying to make my mother look like one of those guys in the famous painting of that era. Lori Barger, her physical therapist would do a more modern version of bandaging and this became a real challenge of the bandagers.

On everyone's day off, Winnie and I would keep watch. Changing special underpants, cleaning her and the bed sheet, feeding, giving water, cleaning her teeth, getting the medicines down. It was amazing. She took food and water until the day before she died.

I was living moment to moment. **This is the real lesson.** When we hear 'live each day as though it were the last' or 'live in the moment,' I think we might consider taking heed. I had little choice because it was the only way I could get through.

In between all of this I began to put her papers in order and make arrangements that I would not be prepared to make when the time came. I made lists of all who had to be notified, asked what to expect, and prepared as best I could.

I talked to her about how wonderful it was that she had done such a great job in her life. I said that perhaps we made a contract to come into this life and be how we were with each other to learn. I told her that she had done her job well and that I forgave her for any of the hurts that I felt she had inflicted on me and she forgave me in the same light. We agreed that we should be proud to have finished so well. She was happy and so was I. She loved whenever I told her that story and always said "that is a lovely way to think about things". I told her she was welcome to stay as long as she wanted and I would care for her but she was free to go when she wanted. She had done what she had come to do. I called her sister Helen and asked her to talk to my mother even if my mother could not say much. Her sister spoke of days long ago and my mother heard and was relaxed and somehow soothed by this.

I spoke to her quietly each night and helped her mentally see her husband and her parents and she said she could and it made her happy.

She was in pain and her breathing was very labored as I kissed her goodnight.

At 5:00a.m on April 27th of 2006, I watched my mother free herself from her body. I felt her breath and heart stop. I wanted to hold her hand to comfort her only to realize that she was no longer there. It is like two sides of your mind are working simultaneously. One mind says, Oh, my God, that is my mother turning cold and white and the other side of my mind said no, it is just her shell, she has gone.....and she had.

I had a difficult time trying to get out of my clinical mode and into the reality of what had happened. Each night thereafter I thought and thought about how she and I had been so much a family without anyone else coming forth. People who had been around us at that time never understood the lack of contact that her family had with her. I had moments when I would call Winnie and say "how can this be, what can I do?"

Finally I realized the most important thing for myself. THIS HAD BEEN OUR KARMA TO WORK OUT. We had been alone to do our work. I truly believe that these five years had been for a purpose and because it never felt like a chore and I never once felt resentful (frustration, yes, but resentment no.) I was quite sure I was making a proper assessment.

I felt sorry from time to time for my sister and my mother's grandchildren and her son-in-law because they had a lot of reasons why they could not make time (including, by the way, that I was the gatekeeper and what could they do?) to call or write to her some words of happiness or solace and that in the end they would finally feel the brunt of what had happened. I, would, of course, as it had always been, be the target of all their anger and inabilities. In the end I understand completely and I urge you to learn from my story.

Perhaps your friends or family, boy/girl friends, wives/husbands have, at times of difficulty, tried to put the onus on you by threatening to leave you if you do not do what they want or think you should do or say. Do not be threatened by this. I am in no way implying that if you are derelict in your responsibilities or your behavior that it is acceptable and what follows applies. It does not. However, in most of these instances these people just want their way and they think that their importance in your life is worth more than your integrity and the value of your word to yourself or others. In my opinion, above all things "to thine own self be true" will take you to your bliss on the fast track.

WHAT MAY SEEM TO BE THE LAST STRAW OR THE ICING ON THE CAKE IS ACTUALLY A GREAT GIFT.

Look at your life in this way in all of its aspects and you will find a much different paradigm for your life. Clean up, so to speak, everything you can with those around you who seem like biting fleas and see them as helpers to your growth. Stop all resentment. Do not let anyone **LIVE IN YOUR MIND RENT FREE. LET NO ONE MESS WITH YOUR BLISS.** It takes away from your purpose on your path and most likely has a way of moving into those corners tucked away for resentment and discontent. These feelings hurt no one but you. The others may have their own problems and may, indeed, make YOU the target but PAY NO MIND. These are most often their inability to see clearly or to accept what they are truly incapable of accepting. This does not make them bad or mean or any other name we may have want to apply to them. It just makes them who they are and it is NEVER our place to waste time and energy in judging. Just put your mind to what your purpose is to accomplish and do so.

It is imperative to clean the slate with your parents. They brought you here, perhaps because you had made a prior agreement to work out things unsettled at another time or perhaps to help you expand in your understanding of life and the universe. Be thankful for whatever happened and give thanks to them. Drop the crap and move on in your life. The person who will benefit most is **YOU**.

My second most important advice, in my experience, is that sometimes it is necessary to divorce people. Not in a negative sense. I am not suggesting that you judge or malign them, but better recognize that some issues cannot now or perhaps ever be resolved. You might try everything that you can and in all fairness they may feel they are doing the same, but still no resolve occurs. **DROP IT. LET GO. LOVINGLY DETACH** with the emphasis on **LOVINGLY**. We are never in a position to decide who or what is right or wrong, are we? The many sides of situations and people are too multitudinous to ever begin such a task. All it ever ends up being is our opinion, nothing more.

You may be saying "but how can I divorce my mother or father or brother or sister or son or daughter or whomever?" I say you must detach in a loving way and move on. Without guilt, anger, resentment or any other unnecessary emotion that weighs you down and stops your forward motion. You may say "but they are my family." And I say they are just souls we choose to meet along the path just as they choose to meet us.

When you have learned what you needed from your grade school teacher and moved on to junior high, etc. did you have any of these unpleasant feelings? No! You are grateful and just move to the next level of your education. Love and gratitude are the only answers for,

WHAT YOU RESIST PERSISTS.

DIP YOUR FINGERS IN THE ICING ON THE CAKE AND WALK ON WITH JOY AND CONFIDENCE IN YOUR NEXT CHALLENGE.

My mom Doris with Dante, Lori, me, and Winnie

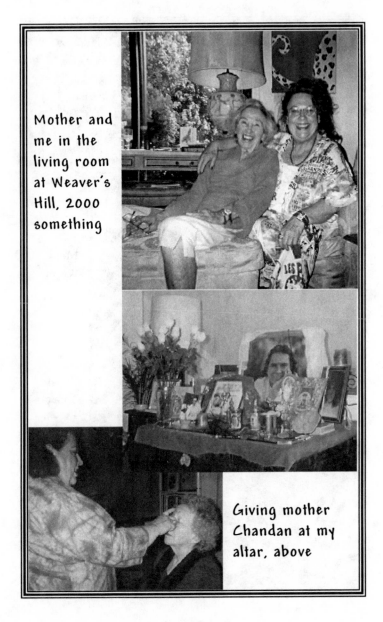

Mother and me in the living room at Weaver's Hill, 2000 something

Giving mother Chandan at my altar, above

Mom, Winnie

Our Friend Joseph <- - - -

Doris, 7 wks before her freedom

Spreading Mom's ashes, May 2007

with Winnie, Margaret Crawford (above) and Rose Adams (below)

Winnie's dog Lettie,
my mother's favorite pal,
and an important member
of our little family

"I'm not afraid of dying... I just don't want to be there when it happens"
WOODY ALLEN

"Next to love, sympathy is the divinest passion of the heart"

EDMOND BURKE

FINDING MY BLISS ONCE AGAIN

So here I go again. When my father died I had a very difficult time. I wore his bathrobe until it was in shreds. I wanted to smoke again and eat lots of chocolate only to convince myself that I would end up a fat smoking sad woman who's father would still be dead. It was different. I was working on the streets with homeless children and time only permitted moments of primordial grief.

Now, my mother passes and I have so much to take care of in that regard that I have not one moment to myself. In between everything else, I grieve my loss and acclimatize myself to the changes. I continue to write this book as often as time permits and to think of ways to start my life again. I had a previously written children's book on stress, hidden away in the dark chambers of my upstairs file cabinet.

I had taken my thirty-year old stress management tape, and re-mastered it into a CD. My dear friend, Mari Cammarano, had helped me to build a beautiful web site, www.MaxineGaudio.com, on which we began to sell the CD, my Reiki work with individuals and corporations and to promote my Reiki classes. I had just finished a large speaking seminar for the top producers of a huge insurance company that had taken me to Scottsdale, Arizona for a few days. My speaking fee is high enough to offset the people not always "getting it" the way I would like. I had created a PowerPoint presentation that I loved and so it was a nice diversion before my mom died. But what could I think of doing that would now help others and still satisfy me now?

I thought that if I were to update and re-master the children's tapes onto DVD and add drawings to it I could help a huge amount of children in stressful situations to have a tool of protection. I spoke with my closest friend and known artist, Winnie Staniford. She had wanted to illustrate a children's book for as long as I had known her. Here, I thought, was the perfect combination. We have already been working together with Reiki both in classes and in corporate programs, so why not this. I had re-mastered before at The Carriage House studio. The owner of this studio, Johnny, introduced me to his friend, Richard Corsello who was known for being a studio engineer both in the music business and in films.

The moment I met Richard I knew he was just the guy to understand what I had in mind. I met him because really, I needed to take the simple digital movie that I had of my mother's 92nd birthday party and make it into a professional

DVD. I had invited all the people she was closest to or had known for her stay with me because I wanted her, without knowing what I was actually doing, to talk about her life and how she felt about things. I wanted her to tell people what she thought while she was alive and for them to tell her how they felt about her under the same circumstances. This, as I discussed with my sister and my Aunt Helen, was to be her memorial service. Why should someone else talk about her when she could talk about her own life? Why should people not be able to say what they want while they are alive? I wanted a celebration of her freedom, not some gloomy service where everyone went away sad and crying. She would never have liked that. She always enjoyed being the life of the party, so why not now?

Richard sat with me in the studio and we discussed what I wanted edited and I added a voice-over to the ending, reading a piece on death by Gibran. He made a phenomenal DVD out of this little piece of mine and so we began to get to know each other. Well, what a joy that was.

We spoke of my idea for children and he thought it was great and would come on as a partner in this venture. He would provide the sound and his other clever ideas. His other gift was a sensible knowledge of marketing these kinds of products.

Oh, good grief, how I do go on. Between all of this and trying to get rested from all the sleepless nights and five years of not really having a life of my own I was trying to get my "genius" back.

One day I am talking with my long time friend Margaret Crawford and she is telling me about how much she hated spending a few hours lay over in Iceland. This reminds me that it was a country I had always been fascinated by and attracted to but had never visited. I had been nearly all over the world. Riding camels in the dessert or wearing a berka or any other type of unusual native dress was not unheard of for me. I had always wanted a kind of adventure, an experience of the world and its people. In my mind it was a sort of visiting of places that felt familiar to me from another time in history. If you have no taste for these thoughts just calm down and move on. I believe that I wanted to go to the places of my other lives and finish whatever Karma was necessary, known or unknown.

One day in July of 2006, I wake up and think, "I want to go to Iceland". I wanted to go and I wanted to go then. I called Winnie and asked if she wanted to go. "Yes" she replied, "I have always wanted to go there." She checked for flights and I looked for hotels and side trips. We voraciously consumed everything we could on history, life, geography, and folklore, and shared it with each other. The Internet became, for the first time, a place of more information (just what I, the information officer, needed.)

I spoke to my client Stephan, who was at that time in Hawaii and in the middle of treatments. I told him I could not be reached at the usual number but gave him the name of my hotel in Reykjavik. He was a lovely, apparently spiritual man in search of the miraculous in his own way. We had wonderful discussions about so many things and his experience with Reiki treatments was extraordinary.

Soon thereafter, Stephan calls me not from Hawaii but from Miami and says he is on his way to his home in Nassau. I think that is where he is heading until I receive a call on the morning of my departure, to hear Stephan saying he is on the flight to Reykjavik and will join us. "Great!" I say, "where are you now?" "In the Miami airport ready to board a flight for New York where I will pick up clothes. I will see you at the airport" he says.

Journey to the Center of the Self

Let the games begin. We are already on a new adventure with no idea or projections on the outcome. All I know is that I desperately need a deep respite from all I have been through and an adventure of this nature is most probably going to provide this, at very least.

We made all the arrangements, did not sleep all night on the flight and arrived in Reykjavik at 6:30 in the morning. You know when you arrive at an airport and you have to adjust yourself? I did not. For the first time in my life I felt immediately at home. I was not in the least tired even after over 24 hours of not sleeping and as soon as our car met us at the airport we were all laughing. The good times had begun. The land on the drive from Keflavik airport to Reykjavik was all of about 35 minutes or so. The scenery was beyond description. It is something you would either love or hate. We all loved it. It was quite like being on the moon in a way. Lots of volcanic rocks, a huge glacier way off over the water standing almost up on the sea like a mystical mountain of ice and snow, a terrain not easy to describe but enchanting all the same.

We arrived at our Hotel 101, a boutique hotel designed and owned by a woman artist. We were escorted to our individual rooms, unpacked, and took a few hours to nap. Remembering that in July it is still summer and considered the "Land of the Midnight Sun", we had NO darkness except from the setting of the sun at midnight until its rising at around 3:00 am. The darkness was more like a slight twilight, if that. We found ourselves staying up for 30 to 40 hours at a time and feeling neither tired nor hungry. We ate of course, great food with lovely service.

We made as much use of our time as we possibly could. In the night I would initiate Stephan in the first degree of Reiki and we would all talk as though talk was a newfound toy. They would eventually go to their rooms and we would all sleep for a few hours until I would feel that time should not be wasted and I would call each room and we would slowly get ready for our next adventure.

How great it was not to be responsible for anyone or have need to call or make contact with anyone outside of our own world. We found a great spa to go to called the Laugar Spa. It was quite modern in many ways. For one, they took a picture of your eye and that was the mode of entry to everything thereafter. You would put your eye up to this little screen and the doors would open to let you into the spa or the pool or the dressing area, whatever.

It was incredibly clean and lovely with sculptures here and there. The lighting was low as in a nightclub yet light enough to be decent. There were many choices of steams, saunas, large Jacuzzi-type pools, showers, and all with different changing lights under the water or overhead in the steams and fantastic different aromas in each venue. The showers smelled mostly of lemon. Very fresh, whether hot or cold. We were enjoying the hot pool when Steph decided that he wanted to try the large wooden barrel of freezing cold salt water. He gave out a hell of a yell and then challenged us to try. Winnie went first, came out and then I went in. My God, it was so cold that I thought my feet were freezing in the few seconds that I was in.

We were having a great adventure just in the spa. We went under that shower in a steam room that had a circle of colored lights in the middle of the foggy room. I closed my eyes and began to chant. Steph and Winnie followed until we all felt we were about to enter a space ship. Most unusual. I was becoming more and more relaxed. I know you are probably thinking that I was becoming completely mad, but no, just relaxed.

Journey to the Center of the Self

We all ran outside and jumped into the pool, heated of course, geothermally from the earth. We swam around laughing all the while and then went to explore several of the hot pots around the pool. We spoke to many people, both alone and with families, until I think we secretly felt we were Icelandic. Perhaps sometime in the distant past we had been.

Winnie was sitting with an Icelandic fellow who of course was completely taken with her. I in the meanwhile was in the larger pool with Stephan who had taken to dragging me around with my head and ears under the water in some method of therapy that he had been experimenting with. I began to chant mantra. First and last it was a huge long Ommmmmm, which I began to realize, was spreading out into the water. From under the water it seemed to resonate in a way I cannot here describe. I just know that I could understand how this vibration could have been responsible for our beginnings. You can most certainly see that I was relaxing my mind in a way that I had not done for many years. I cannot even believe that I am writing about it for you all to hear. Try it for yourself sometime and hear what I heard. Keep your ears under water and use a deep-throated Om sound as you might do if you practice Yoga. It is not as strange or unusual as it may appear to you now.

We decided we would go back inside, relax in the heat and get ready to go. While walking by the inside pool Steph, as was his habit, found his pants falling down so we had another round of laughter.

Although every moment together was like some indescribable event and we really had no need of much else, we had planned a circle tour of the volcanoes and waterfalls and geysers. We were picked up in a huge, and I mean huge Jeep of some sort. The tires were like those of an eighteen-wheeler and I needed a small set of stairs to "mount" the beast of a vehicle. Of course you know Winnie and I were already hysterical with laughter and the driver was already not entirely happy. We picked up an English couple that proved quite brave just to travel with us.

As I turned down the window and Stephan turned to talk to us in the back, the driver took the opportunity to insist on seat belts and windows up. How long could we last?

The driver was really an excellent guide. He knew so much about everything that I lost my usual job as Information Officer, but I was glad I had read so voraciously before the trip. There is no explaining the sights. We fell in love. The landscape ever changing. We went over what seemed like cow paths with holes and rock included. Alongside one could see the volcanic rocks with all of there incredible energy. We were bouncing from side to side and up and down laughing all the way and driving the guide completely insane. By now the windows were slightly open and I had taken off my belt to hold onto the driver's seat. It definitely made for a much calmer ride for me. He was playing some folklore music very low on the radio and I asked if he could turn it louder. Winnie asked for another increase in volume until the drums and Viking-like voices were all-pervasive. Now we felt we were on a Viking ship with the drums beating time for our rowing. Laughter and more laughter.

We arrived at an amazing place where the plates of the earth are separating. I had wanted very much to see these and thought that they would just be small cracks or openings in the ground. No! They were the width of a road with the volcanic walls as high as walking in a valley. I was completely amazed and delighted. We walked for a long distance and then over a few bridges. It was an idyllic scene of both lava walls and green open grasses with flowing rivers of water. Too beautiful to describe. Go there and see.

From there we went jolting again to find ourselves at the base of a huge glacier. We decided to go snowmobiling. We were led to a room and helped to put on "the gear." This consisted of a black nylon type jumpsuit, boots of the same texture, gloves and a helmet. Winnie did not want to drive so I guessed I was the one. I had done this before in Pennsylvania farmland in the snow at night. It was, at the time quite great. Now it seemed a bit more daunting. Oh well, onward we went waddling our way outside the dressing shack to take pictures of ourselves and laugh a little more.

The leader instructed us that it had the potential for danger if we did not follow the course he set exactly by his runners. He explained that there was some melting going on and that there were potential crevasses which if we fell into we could most likely not be able to be retrieved. Dandy! Just dandy! No pressure, oh no. It was beautiful beyond explanation. Both thrilling and frightening. Winnie and I were the only women besides two young girls; the others were all men and ready to conquer. Off we went. I watching like some hawk not to venture off the path, Winnie chanting quietly behind me. Not too much laughing until we came to a place to rest and view. Steph lay back on his machine like a beautiful baby Buddha and the laughter began again. After a while we had a chance to get off and see a crevasse where water was running, and while others lay down to drink the fresh glacier water, I stood thinking they looked like animals in a trough and that it looked a bit thin for me. Win said I looked like a motorcycle cop at the ready to give out tickets. We returned down off the glacier and although it had taken a lot of concentration I wished I could do it again. I would have enjoyed the speed if I could have been in a safe snowy place.

Journey to the Center of the Self

In the days to follow we visited museums, the great city of Reykjavik with all of the wonderful and charming restaurants. We made a day trip to soak ourselves in the magic waters of the Blue Lagoon and dined at a restaurant called Perlan (the pearl) which was in a huge dome overlooking the city and turned 360 degrees while you ate, providing a view of the entire area from up high.

It was such a great time that we all decided to change our tickets and stay a while longer. Stephan mentioned that we were only two hours from London and for a moment or two we all had the fantasy to just keep traveling.

The trip home was wonderful as well. The captain of the Icelandic Air flight kept coming out of the cockpit. Winnie could not figure out why I kept leaning over and watching and not listening to her completely. He was rather handsome and eventually he came over to talk. We discussed that in my misbegotten youth I had flown small private planes. This led to the fact that he had been reading in a newspaper of a man who flew small planes into places around Iceland that had small private landing strips. He gave me the man's name and phone number and we were already planning our return trip.

Once over JFK airport we could feel the heavy and dirtiness of the air. A strange feeling after the lightness of the pollution-free air of Iceland. This, I suppose, was the end of this journey. I felt fantastically renewed. I was full of energy to get started finishing this project.

Within a few days Winnie and I, playing that very same folkloric music we loved in the Beast Jeep (every day, unfortunately) planned and booked our next trip back and in a few days that was all set for November. I was a child waiting for Christmas. The days are still not moving fast enough until we return.

So, lots of work sorting out my mother's business and the work that comes with that. Lawyers, accountant, money manager, etc. and at the same time moving as rapidly as possible to stay on course with some important preparations for a future. I had a great hope of a new beginning and I continue to project my mind in that direction. I suppose I failed to say that at the same time, as my mother's dying the apartment complex that I live in became a condo-conversion. How was I supposed to make all these decisions? I decided to take each day at a time and see where it led. After all was my book not based on living in the moment?

This all lead to a time of mixed feelings. I was fresh and renewed after the trip but still getting over that last five years. I worked, as I continue to do, to compete everything by November. Meanwhile there is a Saga that has already been told in another chapter.

As you may recall, for some years it seemed I had become the Statue of Liberty of my area. Bring me your tired, etc. Many people needed help of one kind or another. This one finding a place to live, another needing a way to get a green card, always a new problem for me to solve. 'Why me', I used to think? I guess I always imagined myself or my child in a foreign country with these kinds of problems and I would have wanted someone to be of assistance.

I had a friend/boyfriend who was Persian and at the time of the hostage problem in his county he found himself stuck here with a sick four and a half year old child with a blood disease. To refresh your memory, there was a lot of commotion owing to my commitment to Amir, Shiva and her mother, Shahla.

At the time of all this commotion, I had a Biofeedback Clinic in Winston-Salem, North Carolina. I wanted to move and because I was also involved in corporate stress management training,

I commuted between there and Connecticut every two weeks. I found a fantastic place to live and eventually made my main residence in Connecticut where I had been born and lived much of my life. The commuting allowed me to take care of my newfound responsibility of my little Shiva.

Let me not bore you with the details. In the end Shiva grew up, went to college in Washington, DC and of course found a way to move her entire family nearby.

This brings me to my next adventure. The Transcendental Meditation group had now formed a great number of people to go to Fairfield, Iowa and Washington, D. C. to "fly" for peace. They called it Invincible America. I received an email stating that we should all consider our responsibility and go to either place to do the Yogic Flying of which I have previously spoken. My friend Kathy Connor in Greenwich encouraged me by going. My friend Dr.

Alarik Arenander, Director of the Brain Research Institute was sending me daily one-liners to push the trip. The news of their success was coming in daily and being written up in newspapers and national magazines. I had to consider because not to go would be hypocritical on my part. Having this ability to make my contribution to peace and not doing it was not the path I was inclined to take.

Shiva and I had been speaking for some years. She and her father came to visit me while my mother was still alive and when my mother died, Shiva begged me to come to D. C. and stay for a while. I could not. I promised that in August I would come down and spend a weekend with her to catch up on all the years. She was now 32 years old and quite the beautiful and intelligent woman I knew she would be. She had been married and divorced but had bought her own condominium and had put her life together better than most people older than herself. Talking with her was always a delight. In some ways, because of her philosophical beliefs and her love of many other things, we had a lot in common.

How long winded this feels to me so I hope you are hanging on. I talked to Winnie, who also does the Yogic Flying and we decided to go to D. C. and participate. I spoke to Shiva and she kindly invited us to stay with her. This allowed me to spend time with her and fulfill my desire to do my part.

As you have come to expect, this led us to another, although small yet not insignificant, adventure of sorts. We took time to see a little of D. C. I loved the energy in the capital. We went to the Kennedy Center. From the top you can see the whole of Washington. We were tired but happy. While waiting for Shahla to get the car, I saw a beautiful woman in a fabulous sheer black coat come out of the building I was standing in front of. I stopped her to ask about the coat. She said she was married to a man from Saudi Arabia and had purchased it there. I asked her if there was anyplace I could locate one in this town and she told me where to go. She said they secretly called it the Terrorist Strip Mall. I was really laughing now. I suppose it carried this name because it had any number of Middle Eastern stores and restaurants there.

We were all tired now, needed to get food, and so we left it for another day.

I suppose I have failed to add the most important factor. Shahla, Shiva's mother, lives in the same building as she does and her father in the building across the street. This became a real family reunion in which Winnie had an opportunity to see the people I had discussed through the years, and the family and I had a chance to make all our forgiveness's, etc. It was, a great opportunity to begin again to know people who had been such a large part of a time in my history. I suppose the same for them. Altogether, it was a time without a lot of sleep that proved to be a wonderful time for all of us.

On the day before we were due to leave, we decided to go to Alexandria, Virginia and then to this mysterious shopping mall. We had to do all of this in time to meet Shiva's new boyfriend so time was of the essence. We finally found the place. I had a great pulling to go to this particular restaurant before going to the store to buy the coat. I have no idea why it had to be this place, but it did. We indulged in great food and I, of course, talked to many people. A man entered the place dressed in a bow tie, striped shirt and suspenders. Quite the gentleman. People were smoking tobacco through hookahs, the Middle Eastern water pipe and eating and talking. This particular gentleman turned out to be an architect and very interesting. He said after that he did not know why he had come in because he was not hungry. He had gotten out of his car and into his car twice and then felt so drawn to come in.

FINDING MY BLISS ONCE AGAIN

We spoke privately after and he explained that he was having a difficult time. Very lonely and unsure of what he wanted to do and that he was very grateful that I had come along to talk to him and help. I, in my usual ridiculous way, suggested that he meet the new husband of Shiva's mother who was a builder. They have since met and we will wait and see. I suppose even at a time I least expect, I am called upon to do some unusual work. It is always a pleasure to serve the Divine. After all, what is my job here anyway?

We ate in wonderful restaurants day and night. It was just like the travels of my youth. I had spoken so many times of these kinds of foods and people and customs that finally I had a chance to share them with my closest friend. What a pleasure it was. Exhausted but happy we made our way back home. Sorry to leave but happy to be back in our own homes and our own beds.

What will be the next adventure? What will be my new path? I only can have faith and keep my promise to live each day at a time and surrender as best I can. Faith at difficult turns in the road and times of unsurety are not easy but I must be true to my own words because I believe they are true.

I have found my patterns, done my energy work, and begun to surrender.

And this brought, in the beginning of November 2006 yet another trip to Iceland. This was to be a scouting trip to see if we could, indeed, find work and determine if we had just been in a dream or if we really were being drawn to live and work in Iceland part of the year. We had a few business meetings with people that we thought would be appropriate for our work. I was interviewed by a journalist, Johann, who had a radio program on Radio Saga. He was interested because we were going to return in March to begin working at the Laugar Spa, a part of the well known

World Gym. Following this we spoke with a woman who had a hotel at the base of a Snaefellsnes Glacier on the Snaefellsnes peninsula where we were considering doing our energy work retreats. Everything went very well. We set out schedules and will let the Divine work out the details.

On November 20th of this year my Reiki Master Ivan Bakic will be returning with a new energy. He has spent some many years between India and Croatia receiving and working with a higher form of energy, which he is planning on coming to share with me. I look forward to this, as he is always present when I am ready for new beginnings.

WISH US LUCK BECAUSE WE WILL SURELY NEED IT.

Winnie in Blue Lagoon - Iceland 2006
The famous Gullfloss waterfall in Iceland

2006
Winnie on the
glacier before
snowmobiling

Max
traveling to the
glacier for
snowmobiling

below, with
Stephan

Viking girls in Iceland

Steph & Max on the drive to the Blue Lagoon July 2006

Outside the Perlan Fall 2006

Nov. 2006 in the cave again with Sol

*"Life is like riding a bicycle. To keep your
balance you must keep moving"*
ALBERT EINSTEIN

AND AGAIN IN ICELAND

November came and so did Ivan Bakic and Gressi, the son of my friend in Iceland, Solveig and so many others. We had a houseful of people on and off from just after Thanksgiving until the end of January 2007. It is so involved that it is difficult to begin at all. As I write now, it is March of 2007 and I have been back in Iceland for some many weeks and will most probably finish this chapter back in the USA and most probably on April 27th, the one-year anniversary of my mother's passing. Perhaps for your sake, you the faithful reader, I will begin from the time that Bakic came off of the plane from Croatia.

Winnie and I (I am sure you remember her because she is my partner in crime so to speak. At least most of our escapades are together and most certainly not entirely by chance.) made our way to the airport with great excitement to meet Ivan. Winnie because she had heard about my Reiki Master for so many years and with the idea that we would be three generations of Masters all together and I just because I had not seen him in almost 12 or more years. He had been so excited on the phone about our reunion and he was looking forward to passing on the much higher frequency energy that had been passed to him.

He came off the plane looking much as before and we picked up just as though time had stood still. Arriving home we made him comfortable in his room and being on a different schedule we all talked and went to bed.

Our time from then on was about his resting and my planning what he wanted as a work schedule. We laughed and talked and meditated together and the old routine with a slight variation began. Me on the phone making arrangements, Ivan trying to get his computer in order and Winnie and I working on getting everything into one day at a time. He was fixated on getting the proper attachments for his computer to work and a new printer, and, and, and. Winnie was starting to get the idea of how it had been so many years before and I was more than delighted to have some help this time. Ivan gave the personal treatment schedule for Winnie and me and so it went. There was huge energy in our meditations and the same in our treatments. All the while having to cook, drive, greet incoming and outgoing people coming for his new treatments, running his astrological charts in time for his "readings" and explaining to everyone, all the while entertaining him and the people.

We celebrated Thanksgiving together with much fun but we were all slowly being affected by the ever-increasing frequency of the energy building in the house. I was still talking to Gressi in Florida and he was planning on coming to Connecticut within the next few weeks. In between the three of us were talking astrology, energy, personalities, treatment results, old times and everything else that you could think of. Everyday dragging ourselves up to eat, meditate, meet and treat. In between there were drives to New York to leave him for a few days or a week to do readings, treatments and seminars there.

By Christmas we were a little "fried crispy." Gressi drove for two days (just like a Viking) and arrived into the mix. It was so nice after months to put a face to the voice. He was here to work with Ivan and me and I was working on finding him a job to help him change his life. In the first few days there was a fair amount of tension and the house was now filled to the brim. All beds were now spoken for.

No need for all the details. It would fill another small book. The culmination of all this came around the time of the end of 2006 and into the evening of New Year's Eve and a few days following. I must inject one small incident of importance. On the day before Christmas and before Gressi had arrived, Ivan gave me my last initiation into one of the new energies. I had already had way more than anyone else of his "gold" treatments. I was, once again, the guinea pig for his energy treatments. My experiences were nothing less than Divine but if I recount them you will surely make the decision that I was a few sandwiches short of a picnic (a little out of my mind) but it was and is not true. This was a time of great importance in my life.....another paradigm shift....another level of consciousness.....an experience of surrender not just in thinking but an integration of mind, body and spirit.

Just after the initiation Ivan and I sat in front of my altar and communicated without too many words. We both felt on fire in a way that one can only understand if they have had the experience. He left and went downstairs and I called Winnie to come up. Together we sat talking about how high the energy had become and how we were almost feeling an out-of-body experience. The intensity became so great that I felt we should go downstairs. We did and I somehow explained to Ivan that I felt that I had been given more initiations. He only replied with a simple hmmmm as was becoming his way when he was unsure of exactly what was happening.

In the evening we went for dinner at a restaurant for Christmas Eve that was owned by one of my clients. We were hungry beyond normal and amazed that we could have made the drive. By now I was really feeling the power of what had happened and I realized that we were all in an altered state (not to say that we had not been living in one but this was greatly increased.)

Try and jump back with me now. It is the day of New Years Eve and I have asked my dear friend and student, Arona, to come and be with us for this special event. I initiate Gressi who appears to have no idea of the sacredness or importance of what is going on. No matter. Things go great. He and Arona begin to practice the Reiki together. Both are satisfied with the results. Ivan, Winnie and I are all somewhere out of this world. We would lie around, listen to music, and talk with Gressi about what he is experiencing and finally, eat and go to bed. I cannot believe the experience that I had during the time of initiation. Everything from this time on is more powerful than I have ever experienced. Ivan is drunk with energy although never willing to admit it, his half-closed eyes and sharp tongue have always been the indication to me that he is.

The following night I lit the entire house in candles. Arona had brought candles especially designed for Gressi's issues and we gathered in the atelier in front of the altar to begin the last of the four initiations. It was so beautiful with the candlelight and the gathering of three generations of Reiki Masters all together to perform this initiation. Arona was not able to be there for this final event because Ivan felt it was too much energy for her at this point.

Following the initiation I explained to Gressi, as I had done each time, what I had seen. If he related he certainly did not share it but no matter, we had all had a life-altering experience together. What a way to begin the year.

Some time went by and I was beginning to feel a huge amount of a new kind of purification. I was breathless, unable to do much, moving from freezing cold to hot and again to cold. My stomach felt hungry every few hours although I had no appetite to go with it.

I had many hours of feeling as though I was not totally in my body and then I was told to start drinking green tea and other cooling foods to help the fire in my body to cool. I needed to bring my physiology back to where it belonged. I had a huge amount of energy and I had to adjust myself to the new level of consciousness that I was vibrating to whilst continuing to bring myself back into my body and this world, so to speak. The cold, of course, was coming from the fact that my energy centers (chakras) and the Kundalini energy highly provoked and moving all too quickly through my spine was like being on fire or having a fever without really having a fever. This then, was the cause of the constant chills.

It was necessary for Winnie to stay and take care of me. She cooked and kept everything including me and herself going. I must say that was quite an ordeal as she also had taken a huge amount of treatment and had a long exposure to the high frequencies infused

in the house. We both had times when
we wondered what would become of us
and how we would ever get back to
Iceland to keep our work commitments in
March. It was a great experience and
gave us both a tremendous new ability to
help others heal. It was also a time of
really learning to keep the commitment
of **surrender** and altogether it was a very
scary proposition. If only we had
someone to tell us what was REALLY
going on. Now, however, we know and
better still we know how to help others in
their quest for spiritual freedom without
all the extreme experiences.

We both had blood tests for Dr.
Dulin who found that they were very odd
indeed. For him it was as new as it was
for us. We felt that we were purifying
our entire systems. He thought the same
but felt that I particularly was at risk
with my kidneys and wanted to take time
to decide what to do to help the situation.

As it goes in life, we both got ourselves collected enough to leave for Iceland on the first of March.

It was our intention to stay for six weeks during which time we would start work at the large spa that we had contracted with in November of 2006. We had decided to stay at our favorite Hotel 101 which we loved and where everyone was like family for us. Our friend Johanna took care of our every need allowing us to rest and then work. She also always kept our same rooms overlooking the mountains and the ocean and the harbor. These had always been our favorite things to view each morning and evening. The guys in the restaurant always put up with our whims and laughed with us a lot. Altogether it has always been a wonderful hotel experience while really feeling like coming home.

But not everything began that well. The man who had contracted with us in November was out of country for the entire time of our visit and his wife with whom I had been in constant email contact was not available by phone or email once we reached Iceland. Too long and unpleasant a story to spend time on and not one necessary to ever talk about again. **Winnie and I learned everything we needed to know about how we had to do business in the future.** Shocking but not without reward when I look back and see how we were slowly guided into the right direction.

I have also failed to mention that sometime in the end of January Winnie and I were talking about how we needed an international lawyer and how great it would be if my old friend in Florida were around. He had started as a volunteer for my Kids with Kids program and then become a meaningful friend. At least I had become one for him and over the fourteen years that I had known him he would call whenever he had a problem.

I had begged him along with his father not to marry this woman he was so crazy about in Miami.....and crazy is the key word here. When I knew him he was a prosperous and brilliant lawyer with at least seven languages at his disposal. He never listened to either his father or me and he married, suffered and finally lost everything including himself. He had moved to Miami and on one of our trips there we met him in an effort to help a little. We always seemed to have some strange connection and whenever we revisited either by phone or in person it took on a major energy. When I tried to help him follow his dream of returning to practice in New York he became unsure that he could once again succeed.

My most famous story about this guy is that he called me at least four or more times every day for months. On a Saturday afternoon he called and said he was going for a haircut and would call later. He never called again. It has always been one of my favorite stories. **"I am going for a haircut and I'll call later"** became a saying that always made us laugh. Well, later never came until the night Winnie and I in our conversation thought perhaps he could help us by answering a few questions. **BIG MISTAKE!** He returned the call a few days later mentioning that he had been too embarrassed to call during the previous two or three years. Ok, no problem, I thought. He answered our questions after looking up some laws and then began calling every few nights and talking for hours. It had all begun again. The intensity of our unusual relationship was about to set sail before someone could come and save me by dragging me off the ship.

He had spent these years reviewing his life and himself. He was most compelling in his stories and I responded with my form of philosophical ideas. I enjoyed his brilliance, his humor and the intensity of the connection. It was not unlike a hot wire exposed in the street....**NOT TO BE TOUCHED**.

But no, I could not leave well enough alone. We had always been magnetized and this time it was to end up out of control. He once again wanted to come to New York and try to start his life again and I, always there to save the day, or as my friend says "swoop and save", offered him a ticket to come and visit for a few days and see how he fared going to the city, etc. I offered him my home to live in so he could get adjusted and his friend in New York told him he could have office space.

Let me cut to the chase. We spoke every night until Iceland and every night while I was in Iceland. It was always exciting and always a very high level of communication. The only real problem was that he hooked into me in a way that I knew everything he was doing and what he was feeling....even when I did not want to. It became a grand experiment with all my idealism and all my old patterns. The bottom line was that we were looking forward to seeing each other again when I returned home. He always mentioned how far away I seemed in Iceland. I never really understood what the difference was talking from Greenwich or from Reykjavik. All I new was that I was once again holding someone up at my expense.

He never came when I returned and he never called nor did he return the ticket and I am sure he was not going for a haircut. This was a time of learning very big lessons and letting go of the past patterns once and for all. The funny thing was that he was not at all like my unavailable parent but much more like my father and therefore much more like me.

So what, it was a great disappointment to say the least. But it was a fantastic lesson. Even though I was, in a way, detached, I felt great emotions whenever he said he missed me or loved me. Now, thanks to that experience, I am free. This will never happen again in any way. No more feeling that I must help or save or "be there" and that it is my obligation as a healer.

With this piece in place I will continue with the chain of lessons learned and the Karma released during this time. All that energy work was taking its perfect course and doing its job all the while honing me more for the tasks ahead.

I had contracted on the Internet to take an apartment in the center of town. This would bring down the cost of our trip and allow us to really experience life as though we lived in Reykjavik. We had hoped that we could shop and cook for ourselves in an effort to get a feeling of being a regular Icelandic living and working like everyone else rather than living life in a hotel, ordering room service or making our daily visit to the fabulous restaurants available in the city.

Journey to the Center of the Self

It all sounded perfect on paper but in reality, well, let me say that things did not go exactly as planned. The apartment was lovely and the owners even lovelier. We had similar interests and the husband, amongst his many other talents, did cranio-sacral treatments. The wife, a fabulous woman, was a designer in the theatre. How perfect. We joined them for the opening of the National Art Museum exhibit and planned to move in the days following.

Well, what to say. We went to see the apartment and although completely charming it would never have worked for us. We were, we found, unable to work and also take care of the daily routine by ourselves. It would just take too much energy. Now Winnie and I needed the balance of work AND rest. Another big lesson that we both had always had a problem with.

We had wanted to go out to the glacier at Snaefellsnes and stay a night or two at the Hotel Budir. Our friends

Solveig and Bryndis made the arrangements and we took the three-hour drive with our favorite driver, Omar. It was snowing much of the way and all the mountains were blanketed in deep snow. Breathtaking hardly describes the experience. We traveled through a new tunnel that took us under the deepest part of the ocean, which was in itself an exciting new event. This was only the beginning.

Omar took us as far up the glacier road as we could go in the weather. We found ourselves in a "white out" and I could hardly hold back my child-like feelings. I had to get out of the car and feel the whole thing. The energy was higher than I have ever experienced in any place outside of a building or room. I understood how fast you could become disoriented and get lost but it was somehow very inviting and thrilling.

We turned around, not without it's own risk and drove down to Budir. Omar left us and we checked into this fabulous country hotel in the middle of all the exquisite energy. We met Ulli, the Manager, who showed us around the entire hotel, had a little late lunch, talked a little business, gave him a treatment and just enjoyed the indescribable views.

It was the beginning of a big storm and Winnie and I decided to go walking in the storm near the ocean. Of course we were laughing all the way, trying to walk into the strong winds. I don't think I will ever need Botox as long as I walk into those kind of natural forces of nature. My face was frozen and no lines could possibly form. We returned to the hotel and waited for our friends to arrive from Reykjavik. Rather than talk about it any more I will just invite you to look at the picture included in the book and enjoy.

Let me not fail to mention what happened next. Once back in Reykjavik I was interviewed again by the well-listened to journalist Jóhann Hauksson who has a radio program called

Morgunhaninn. I was heard again on Saga Radio talking about my work and what it could do. This began the next possibility. He introduced me to the owner of the radio station and she agreed that I would have my own show on a Sunday afternoon for one hour. I had to find an interpreter. I had a fabulous client, Adda, and she had a massage teacher in her school that was willing to take that job on.

Fjola, the woman who became my interpreter was just the perfect person for the job. She understood not only what I did with energy work but also shared my spiritual philosophy. Could I have asked for much more....NO! My program began and I started to discuss the problem of stress and overwork that exists in Iceland as well as how this works with my Unavailable Parent theory. The phone began to ring and ring until all phone lines were busy. Everyone had a question and wanted to meet me privately. There were so many calls that I was asked to do another hour. I did, and for the week following I was inundated with calls and clients.

I was told I could have my own show each Sunday, which I expect to do on our return in June of 2007.

Because my interview with Johann had brought people for treatments I had to find a space for Winnie and me to work. One morning I was awaked by a woman saying that she had found us space just up the street from our hotel (we never moved to the apartment) and that she was arranging for me to be on a very heavily watched TV interview show. Well, I thought, who the hell is this woman talking as fast a machine gun and where did she come from and why was she going to help us? Johanna had apparently made the arrangement and so we met Sikka at the place where we would eventually see our clients.

Winnie was doing auric portraits while I did psychic readings followed by energy treatments. It was great and each stone in the way was being removed one by one. **Each lesson was being learned and we were being moved from one great opportunity to another.**

Now comes the good stuff. Winnie and I had been spending time both thrilled by our opportunity to help so many people and a bit discouraged that we had to wait so long and spend so much of our money not doing what we had made the trip for. This was combined with emails from my lawyers in Connecticut about my twenty-two year court case which my husband once removed (ex) and his dear friend had continued to keep going (the case was being heard in the second circuit in New York), waiting to see what would happen with my apartment complex which was in the middle of a battle between the new owners who were trying to condo-convert and the seniors who were at risk of eviction or 100% increase in rent, the realization that we had been living for nearly six weeks in a very expensive hotel, my son Dante emailing me that "we are unexpectedly expecting", working on the settling of my mother's estate (which involved the constant effort of reaching the endlessly unreachable lawyer handling it all) and most of all making efforts to keep ourselves going with all the after effects of the Winter's energy experiences.

Somehow after each morning meditation together we would be so "spaced out" that we had to push each other to move to our individual rooms and get showered and dressed. All the while receiving the emotions from my Florida friend and spending way too much late evening time talking on the phone with him. With a time difference of five and then four hours it was always after midnight or later before I would begin to prepare to sleep.

In the last two or three days left.....right up until one hour before our departure to the airport the most incredible path opened up wide for us.

I had met a man on the security line on our July 2006 trip who was very charming and most importantly very mentally quick and smart. We had talked at warp speed for about thirty minutes, exchanged cards and humor; he left the lounge for London and Stephan, Winnie and I went on our way to New York. I never gave it much though again, although from time to time we would exchange short emails as one does.

Before leaving on this trip I sent him a note saying that I would be in Iceland in March. He replied that he would be there as well and would let me know when he arrived. That was that....so I thought...even when he emailed me that 'the eagle had landed' (my words)....I sent him my Icelandic phone number and continued the routine of working and planning what we could do to work with the ideas I had created for the original spa.

With few days left, we were shopping for gifts, having dinner with our friends and getting our too many suitcases packed. In the gift store my phone rings. "Where are you?" says the man's voice. "In a store" I say and "Where are you?". "In the lobby of your hotel". "I will be right there." I say. I finish at the cash register and quickly make my way down the street to my hotel.

There he is sitting as regal as can be, just as he was in the airport. Winnie and I talk to him. He and I are talking at our usual high speed about what he is doing and what I want to do. I ask if he can help me and ask him to take a seat on one end of a long couch. I go to the other end and begin a six-minute mental treatment. Time is up and he is remarking on how good he feels. "How do you do that remote control?" he asks. I explain and he makes a call, does not get through, says that he will call later and leaves.

Winnie and I are waiting to be picked up by Jóhann to go to his house for dinner and to meet his wife and family. While waiting in the lobby my phone rings again and I am told to call a woman at the Nordica Spa. I had taken a week to learn the name Hrafnhildur a name that does not sound as it looks (nor does it contain the proper Icelandic letters because they do not exist in our alphabet) and now, in a moment's notice I am told to call Ragnheidur. I write the name and number on a small envelope, rush into the waiting car, beg my friend to keep pronouncing the name for me while I dial the number and say, I hope perfectly, "Ragnheidur, this is Max." We make a time to talk on the following day.

We have a fantastic dinner surrounded by wonderful people who make us feel as though we have been together for years. Winnie and I give energy treatments to them and we talk and laugh until way too late. I make it back to my room just in time to get my evening phone call and finish my last minute packing.

On the morning of the following day we have an early meeting with the head of sales for all the Icelandair hotels. I give her my press kit and we talk about what we would like to do and how we could help people from all over the world by bringing them to Iceland on a spiritual retreat in the land of fire and ice.

Some people are dropping by to say good-bye and then I call Ragneheidur. We talk and she is not only interested but also excited and we make arrangements to email when I arrive back in the US.

All the way to the airport with Omar all we can do is talk about how things happen just the way they are supposed to and how grateful we are that the Divine has just led us around by the nose until we finally could see what was happening. Can it be true? If the original plan had been followed I never would have had to ask for help and this expansive opportunity to serve would never have happened. We remind ourselves on the plane that we must always remember to SURRENDER and TRUST.

I am going to end now because although this is just a spit in the ocean of what has happened throughout my life, I could continue each day to write some fantastic happening. There are few days without their drama and tests. Enjoy all of it because it is only an illusion, a play, and yet an all too important one, indeed.

Not to leave you hanging, however, we have since written several proposals and it is expected that in June of 2007 we will begin our test program with Nordica Spa. They will be the first to offer not only a gym for one's body but also a means to build and expand one's mind and spirit.

Why my soul lies in Iceland

Outside my window at Budir April 2007

Sol, Bryndis on our way home from Snaefellsness

Dear Fjiola, my translator

1st "MasterMind" on Radio Saga

April 2007

My client Adda, & Adda owner of Saga Radio

"You don't live in a world all alone...
your brothers and sisters are here too"
ALBERT SCHWEITZER
ON ACCEPTING THE NOBEL PRIZE

*"To know what is impenetrable to us
really exists, manifesting itself as the
highest wisdom and the most radiant
beauty"*

ALBERT EINSTEIN

REIKI, ENERGY, OR HOW TO FIND YOUR BLISS

I am beginning this chapter by giving you the five basic healing principles by which all Reiki practitioners are expected to follow:

JUST FOR TODAY I RELEASE ALL WORRY.

JUST FOR TODAY I RELEASE ALL ANGER.

I SHALL EARN MY LIVING WITH INTEGRITY.

I SHALL HONOR EVERY LIVING THING.

I SHALL SHOW GRATITUDE FOR ALL MY MANY BLESSINGS.

Reiki (ray-key) is a holistic healing art that originated in ancient Tibet. This both hands on and hands off technique of energy transfer gently helps to restore balance to the body, mind and spirit. The word Reiki means universal life energy ("rei") brought through personal energy ("ki). Reiki is an effective method to promote relaxation, reduce stress, and accelerate the body's natural ability to heal from physical and mental ailments.

The Usui System of Reiki was developed in the 1800's by Dr. Mikao Usui who rediscovered the ancient healing technique in the Sanskrit scriptures of Tibetan Buddhism. Dr. Usui dedicated his life work to the practice and teaching of this natural healing technique. The Usui System of Natural Healing is not a religion and requires no particular belief system.

A Usui Reiki practitioner has been trained in time-honored techniques to facilitate and direct the flow of universal life energy to themselves and others. The practitioner serves as a conduit, helping to channel and focus positive healing energy to the recipient. Reiki works in conjunction with, and as an effective adjunct to medical treatments and other therapies.

Reiki can do many things including relieving pains and acute symptoms, in many cases, quite rapidly....sometimes in moments. I use it more for helping people with their personal issues, mental or emotional issues, if you will, because the energy has a very positive influence on spiritual growth.

Much of my work tends to be working on the mental and emotional issues people have after I have helped them to see the PATTERN of their life overall. After I have verbally or psychically gotten to the core of their life pattern, I am able, with the use of the energy, to help individuals have a much clearer and deeper insight into the particular questions, problems or situation that they might be facing. This in turn helps them to make a quality change, a more correct change and far better decisions in their life, which is why they come to me in the first place. This is what I believe every practitioner or Master should focus on for each individual.

High frequency energy affects each person differently and yet after many years of this work I most often find a common experience between people.

Energy used up in our "merry-go-round" life can be easily replaced, to take away the feeling of exhaustion or being drained, which results ultimately in an imbalance, which over time will most certainly adversely affect you either physically, emotionally or mentally. High frequency energy or Reiki can balance this problem. So many people today suffer from very high stress symptoms such as headaches, digestive problems, colds, lowered immune system or even weak organs that have been overloaded.

So many people are unaware that they are using up life force energy, which can quite simply be replenished through this work.

This would then lead them to be as healthy inside as they are looking for when working out in the gym to help their physical appearance.

When you receive these kinds of treatments or you take part in a Reiki seminar your emotions may often be profoundly affected. Emotional "blocks" are often released and you come into closer contact with feelings that you may have suppressed in the past. Many of my clients, if not most, have deep sadness or anger that has not been accepted. They have stored it away. Suppressed these and other feelings. Experiences change our brain. Beauty, pain, joy, etc. are all imprinted in some physical form in the nervous system.

When you think or feel, different brain cells fire together and the "synapse", the method the brain uses to send information from one cell to another, becomes stronger This would then be a major factor in retaining unconscious patterns.

Experience is always changing your brain, which is not, indeed a solid thing like a piece of stone, but more fluid as a river or stream flowing and changing. Things such as food, emotions, exercise, etc. all change the brain. During stress parts of the brain are provoked to the old cave man instinct called "fight or flight" and in the end, after more and more stress, parts of the brain are in a sense, caused to fragment. The human brain is said to be constantly changing to the degree that, it is said by researchers, that 70% of our brain cell connections (synapses) change every day.

Once you become aware openly with these thoughts and emotions from past experiences and accept them and let them surface not as flaws but only as emotions and feelings that must be given attention and expression, you begin to change your process of thinking. In most cases you have struggled with these things for many years.....even most of your life.

Energy work supports you in your spiritual growth. Those who use this means can better themselves by opening up to higher levels of consciousness, intuition, and much greater self-awareness. My goal with my clients is almost always this and more. I want to help people to become their AUTHENTIC SELVES by finding their patterns, doing the energy work to un-block and release and then helping them to understand the principle of **surrender**, everything that I have been addressing throughout this book. By doing this work in one way or another, and I think this is the most rapid method, a person avoids spending their entire life believing all the "junk" they have heard, and stay forever crystallized in wherever they decided to stop growing and self-exploring.

With Reiki and this kind of healing work the most important thing to think about for me is that once you have found your pattern or patterns in your life, energy work will, given the desire to change, give you the power and energy to act and think with responsibility in terms of making the changes that are so necessary to each of us if we ever expect to break or change these patterns.

This is the only way that you AND the world can even possibly think of making a change in the direction of peace and tranquility. If you think of yourself as that little stone that you used to skip over the water and how many ripples that little stone made to the surface of the water you will understand completely how changing yourself and the innermost core of your being can create a vibration of change to all the surfaces of life around you. Small ripples of self-change just making all the difference not only in you but also in others around you and so on.

All of the work I have spoken about throughout this book is meant to show you the power of love and positive thought. Energy work in conjunction with the other principals in this book is really an expression of self -love and in turn, love and understanding and compassion for others. This is "tuning" your heart, which in turn generates healing and a stronger intuitive ability. The why to this question is that energy is working on a non-verbal thought wavelength that also is capable of, particularly in those people who have worked on growth of consciousness, telepathy.

I love to go to the opera. Besides the feeling of experiencing the distant past.... as though looking though a window to history....and of course the extreme beauty of staging and costuming, I always have felt a deep healing from the sound that emanates through a well trained human instrument. I have been going to the opera, thanks to my family's love of the arts, since around 5 or 6 years of age. Now and for some years I have put Pythagoras' ideas of sound and color together very clearly.

Sound, as in music, is a pure vibration. For myself, I have been known to quietly tear up from the experience of the great voices creating vibrations that most likely I receive in my energy centers (chakras for those who study Yoga or just know.) I often think that different music affects different energy centers. I learned in my classes in Vedic recitation that sacred sounds such as mantra or even recited prayer have the power to create higher meditative states or even this kind of experience for those who have not ever had this happening. It creates a feeling of **BLISS**, and quite frankly, is this not what we are all quietly clamoring for?

Sounds such as mantra and other sacred sounds have vibrations or resonance, which in turn evokes or activates these energy centers that I speak of.

To explain healing with the mind I must explain in a little bit of a complex way. Let us say that the healer mentally constructs the unity of the healer, patient, and the universe losing sense of egos....because of the interconnectedness of David Bohm's non-local quantum potential, time or distance is irrelevant. THOUGHT can unite all allowing phase harmony entrainment and allowing the patient's body to re-establish its normal state of health.

In layman speak, we would say that when a trained healer has the intention and then connects with the patient by allowing the energy of the Universe to enter into him or herself followed by directing that energy it will allow the patient, if they are so willing, to re-establish a state of harmony in his mental and/or physical condition. If we think of ourselves as energy fields or a series of many electromagnetic fields or just billions of sparkling stars organizing ourselves into what we call a body, then we can understand....well, at least try to understand a little better.

As I say to my patients....imagine going to the movies....we see a full-uninterrupted picture but in reality this is a piece of filmstrip being passed in front of the light. We do not notice the gaps between the frames, just the whole picture. This is exactly how the body is. It and everything around us is constantly moving molecular structure.

Let me give you a simple and yet unusual example of the non-time space idea. I have, for many more years than I should say, had a friend with whom I connect and reconnect. Somehow, each time something important is happening in his life he seems to appear to think of me and call. I have seen him through the great and the difficult....mostly the difficult times in his life.

My Florida friend has, as I have told him, been a knowing seducer of my soul. What do I mean? We have always had a connection that for all intent and purpose appeared to be like a non-verbal plug-in. When he thought strongly about me I always knew what was going on and that it was he reaching out to me. Thus enters the time/space issue. We do not live near each other nor do we see each other often and yet the connection is always there. If he wants to speak to me, I know. If he is feeling completely connected to me on a soul level, I know. No doubt, I know. As though the unseen cords were tied together and communicating.

At the end of March of 2007 and continuing on, I connected in this way with someone on whom I have been doing energy treatments. It has been quite surprising to me as the Divine put him in my path almost a year ago and I immediately felt one of those "I have known you forever" sensations. We had no substantial conversation or communication, for that matter, until we met again in the spring.

Having had this experience only twice in my whole life I questioned the purpose of each of them. I have, as of late, come to see that there is a very important reason for this kind of connection but let me finish my point.

When you lose your ego, even for a short amount of time and let the energy come though you....and this is rarely done with surface knowledge, that is to say it is most probably more subconscious. Whatever it is, you allow yourself to connect that energy to another and thus a healing for that person can occur. It is Divine energy in the case of Reiki or high frequency channeled energy, not personal energy.

Healing with the hands involves a similar situation. The healer mentally constructs a union with the oneness of all. Biogravitons mix with gravitons forming a solid bridge or connection allowing phase harmony entrainment. A link is established between the patient and the harmony of the universe, which contains the knowledge, or "vibrations," to re-establish a normal state of health.

If this appears a lot more complicated than you are interested in, then pass it by and pick up where your interest leads you. These small "Quantum" moments are for those, like myself, who like some kind of scientific explanation so we do not feel that it is all some strange and unhinged thinking or just something you MUST believe in. Not at all! In fact, there is no belief required. When the practitioner or Master begins treatment they are merely opening up their channel to the universe to allow YOU to draw in the energy.

You take what you want or need on a level that you are most likely completely unaware of. It is for this exact reason that with these methods one person does not heal another but allows the energy to be filtered though them to be drawn in quantities that the other person wants or needs. Of course I have been often quoted as saying that everyone can draw but not everyone is a Picasso. This means that EVERYONE can do this work but it takes some of us a few minutes and others a few days or even months to affect a change.

This is why I advise you to look for a healer who has a deep talent and understanding of a spiritual life. Not just talking it but actually living each day in the basic principals that I began this chapter with. A Master to me means a person who has mastered their life....ok, ok, not completely, we are not expecting saints, but at least a person whose consciousness is rooted in a strong and healthy foundation of deep wisdom and knowledge. Would you want to learn quantum physics from someone who has never read or studied this science of possibilities? Would you want to learn business techniques from a musician or from a person who perhaps has an MBA (not that such persons might be capable of all?)

While our culture does so little to assist us in exploring at all, let alone more closely, energy **REALLY** is all there is.

Even matter as Einstein's elegant formula ($E=mc^2$) shows, is congealed energy. In other words, energy becomes mass and mass energy. As an example: When you put a log to burn in your fireplace, you are seeing the congealed energy that is the log transforming into roaring flames that are the energy.

The flame could then be transformed into mechanical energy where it might involve a train or run a generator that might, eventually, produce electrical energy.

We say that we sometimes cannot see energy, as in Reiki. Well, can you see germs in the air or microwaves or radio or TV waves? You know that they are there, but can you see them with your naked eye?

Einstein, and you must have noticed that he is/was in some way, my idol, believed there is only a single energy, a "UNIFIED FIELD" which is also spoken of when I speak about meditation and flying, etc., but if so, it has countless faces. Quantum physics, the physics of possibilities, is the principle of increasing dynamism. The core of the universe is pure life and consciousness. Quantum physics has mathematically described our universe as being structured in layers. Underlying all physical reality is the un-manifest Unified Field.

The human mind has the remarkable ability to fathom the finest levels of conscious thought and experience the silent level of the Unified field.

All the great teaching of all the great sages and prophets are, at their roots, the same. Transcend and settle your mind...connect it with its subtle origin and expand.

Think about allowing yourself to move from the superficial to the profound. The Universal field of consciousness is the intelligence governing the universe, **including us.** I learned in classes taken with the Transcendental Meditation Program (TM) what I had learned some time before. It was the necessity for meditation in order to quiet the mind and connect with the Unified Field. I, however, see it (meditation) as the adjunct to energy work, which gives one a well-rounded and continuing way to promote self-enlivening. This fighting our "demons" or calling it the darkness is a totally negative way of programming our minds, when as the TM people say, you can "TURN ON THE LIGHT."

Getting back to my pal (I wish it had been so) Einstein showed through physics what the ancients brought us through the centuries: everything in our material world...animate or inanimate...is made of energy and everything radiates energy. There is a saying in Latin that goes like this: **ESSE QUAM VIDERI.....TO BE, RATHER THAN TO SEEM TO BE.** This seems to fit with Einstein's statement that "reality is merely an illusion, although a very persistent one."

Numerous cultures describe a matrix of subtle energies that support, shape and animate the physical body, called **qi** or **chi** in China, **prana** in the yoga tradition of India and Tibet, **yesod** in the Jewish Kabala, **ki** in Japan and Korea, **baraka** by the Sufis, **wakan** by the Lakotas and the **Holy Spirit** in Christian tradition. You would really have to stretch beyond any place I could go to truly suggest that this is a new idea and that subtle energies do not work along with the material body.

The fundamental law of energy work is when your energy is vibrant, so is your body. The soul is not for many, an easy concept to understand. If spirit, is the intelligent energy of Creation, then can we say that the soul is its manifestation at a personal level?

To work with Reiki is to work with the person's energy and this I feel is to work with the person on a soul level.

I know this might become a bit heavy and serious, but sometimes it has to be that way. Maybe I can give you a moment of change by presenting a case history or two. Perhaps by this means you can follow what happens not just to a theoretical person but also to one who is real and has been through the "slavery" with me. I use the word slavery because it may begin as an enchanting idea and the beginning energy work sometimes appears blissful and lovely and without much personal effort. But no, my dear friends, it definitely is not. For this reason I will first familiarize you with the process of release of all the accumulated thoughts, feeling, perceived negative experiences, etc.

Any kind of energy work is liable to create **purification** in various and sometimes, multitudinous ways. So although it is rarely spoken of I really believe the recipients of this kind of work, including things like massage, reflexology, cranial-sacral work, colonics, certain breath exercises, long intense rounds of meditation and other things of this nature, should be told of the possible experiences that we call purification.

For some, at least following the first few treatments, a person might feel exceptionally well and relaxed. Perhaps some may feel euphoric. Others may initially experience very little, but in time most everyone will feel one or more of the following:

REIKI, ENERGY, OR HOW TO FIND YOUR BLISS

1. Fatigue
2. Irritability
3. Alertness
4. Spaciness
5. Anger
6. Slight disorientation
7. Unusual dreams
8. A feeling that old experiences are surfacing out of nowhere.
9. Physical symptoms such as aches, pains, colds, etc.
10. Places of injury are temporarily painful again
11. A sense that you are not sure exactly what you stand for or what you really believe in or why
12. Increased awareness of self and others
13. A quieting of your mind
14. Compassion for others and an understanding of your relationship to others
15. Difficulty focusing

16. A more realistic sense of self
17. Negative thoughts that seem to come out of nowhere
18. A greater understanding of yourself in the context of your world and where you fit
19. A feeling to search for your overall purpose in life
20. An understanding of why your parents and others came to behave or think as they do
21. Depression
22. Anxiety
23. Fear
24. Sadness
25. Despair

None, some, or all of these purification symptoms may occur. It is most important to detach yourself from them and any outcome of any circumstance. See the difficult symptoms such as fear or anger or worry as an over-lay on the outside of yourself. Watch them but do NOT project them onto others. They are yours to observe and learn from and watch. They are your cell and muscle memories being released. Learn from them but **DO NOT IDENTIFY WITH THEM**. You experienced them once so there is no reason to experience them again. **JUST LET THEM GO. LET THEM BE RELEASED.**

How do you know that this is purification? None of the above mentioned items are liable to stay for any length of time. You might wake up feeling very tired and little depressed or "under the weather." Soon thereafter you might feel just great. Later on in the day some anxiety may surface. **No feeling or experience is prone to last very long. This is the basic and for me, classic, sign of purification.** They are most often feelings that come with no particular relation to anything that is presently happening in your life.

What you can do. I myself do these things and always suggest them to people whom I am working with either as individuals or as a class. Sit on the side of a bathtub, if you have one, and put your feet in a large pot of hot water filled with about 4 to 8 ounces of sea salt. At the same time, scrub your body with a product that contains natural oils combined with sea salt. They are usually sold as body scrubs. Scrub your entire body, back and front, including your face. Sit for a few minutes and then pour out the solution in the pot and take a shower. Do not use soap, just rinse off the scrub.

In the event that you only have a shower at your disposal you may stand in the shower stall and scrub as above following with a rinse off shower only.

Another thing that I do when time does not permit anything taking too long and because I usually do one of these processes any time that I do work on or receive work from someone. I take my normal shower and follow it with a rinse of sea salt in hot water just as I would normally use only for my feet. I do not rinse off.

These techniques are incredibly useful and effective. The salt helps to release the toxins and therefore make the processing easier.

The other thing that I learned from my studies with a Peruvian Shaman for cleaning my space or myself is to go to a local "botanica" if you have one in your area. They are typically found in Latin neighborhoods. There I purchase bottles of a product called Aqua de Florida. It is used in South American countries for this purpose and many others including as a light perfume for men.

Transfer the contents of the bottle or bottles into a spray bottle for ease of use.

I spray my bed before I change my sheets. I sometimes spray myself immediately following my work with someone. I spray my room or rooms when I feel they are not clean on that level. You will find your own use for this product, I am sure.

Leaving the best for last I begin now to share some of my clients' lives with you.

Some years ago I had a practice both in Connecticut and New York. I was referred a lovely fellow who, unfortunately, is no longer here. Close to the time of his death he used to call me and say, "Maxine, I just put a down payment on the farm." He was very old-fashioned for a man just over fifty and used expressions that I had not heard since my grandmother's day.

He came to me in my New York office, which was located on the second floor of a triplex that had an unblocked view of the Hudson River through my many big windows. He was a slight fellow with brown hair and lovely eyes dressed in very casual Eddie Bauer trousers, shirt and a jacket. As I looked at his astrological chart I mentioned to him that although I did not mean to be offensive, I noticed an aspect that led me to feel that he had some kind of a strange sexual situation in which I saw him performing.

I delicately mentioned this to him and he quite bluntly said "Didn't you know that I am a drag-queen?" He mentioned the name by which he was known as he whipped out a photo with himself in a blonde wig, blue cocktail dress, fabulous jewelry and surprisingly, standing next to two very famous New York society women.

I though "gadzooks, what have I gotten into here?" No matter. Not being a particularly judgmental person and not shocked by much if anything (just surprised because of how basic he looked when not in drag) I explained how I would do the mental treatment, what I would be working on and what he could expect. I then rolled my chair across the room, closed my eyes and began the energy treatment. In the first few moments I was looking at this fellow in my mind's eye and he was surrounded with an overwhelmingly brilliant white light. He felt so beautiful to me and so pure and evolved that when I finished I told him what I had seen. Most importantly I never saw him any other way. He was just a beautiful light being for me.

Over time I gave him many treatments, taught him Reiki and stood by him through the good and inevitably, the terrible. For many years he used to say "I don't feel anything, Maxine, these treatments can't be working." But in time he came to know the feeling that accompanied purification to which he attached the idea that the treatments were "working." And so they did, because after a while he integrated both parts of himself and stored the many dresses and wigs and shoes and jewelry.

It was the end of an era for him. He could now express himself without cover of another character.

He always used his Reiki to work on himself. Even near the end he would put his hands wherever he had pain, as I would work on his mental outlook.

He always thought that I was, as he liked to say, "The advanced one" but I think under all the insecurity and sadness it was he who was "The advanced one" and the brave one to boot. He is today one of the few people I actually miss. He had a lovely diamond initial that he wore on the lapel of his cashmere jacket when we once met with my mother in New York. He sent it to me a year or so before he died so he could be sure I would have it to remember him by. Of course I cried, but I wear it still even through it is not my initial. It is a J and when people ask I say it stands for joy.

Then there was my first patient with cancer. It was ovarian cancer to be exact. When I first saw Lois she looked perfectly well and in excellent spirits, but scared, for sure. She was a therapist as well, but had never examined herself close enough to figure out why this was all happening. As I did my reading for her I told her that I felt that her father was a man who had little respect for women and got the feeling that women were of little use. He taught her by his words and actions that as long as she looked good, dressed properly and held herself in upper society situations in a way that would keep him looking good, he would marginally accept her. He pretty much treated his wife with the lack of respect he treated most every human being.

I asked her if both of her husbands had been the same way. She of course agreed. To simplify and shorten the story, I explained that she herself had actually, subconsciously of course, bought into this scenario and had indeed chosen men who represented her father and therefore could try again to have the love of the father that she never felt loved her. Neither of the husbands treated her well. Each one she loved and married helped her to feel less and less that a woman had much standing in the world.

She was an extremely bright woman with a wealth of knowledge about many things, but her underpinnings were faulty. She had suppressed all of her real feelings about herself. She was careful to always say the "right" things and act in a way that was not entirely authentic, to say the least. I believe that she had a great deal of self-hate and unknowingly bought into her father's ideas. She behaved much like her idea of a man. She excelled in her work and in the handling of money. She took on everything as a challenge that must be met perfectly or she would not view herself with much respect. She had to have total control of every situation and viewed other woman with just a bit of disdain unless they were very successful in her eyes.

She had beaten her first diagnosis and was in remission when she came to me. I advised her at that time to be prepared with all the newest research and treatments while she was well so that in the event that she had a reoccurrence she would not have to panic and not know where to turn. She refused to think about it or to follow any of my direction in that instance. I was, however, quite successful in helping her with treatments, to feel much better about herself and to understand much better that she was not only wonderful as a woman but also quite exceptional. This helped her to live much more fully and to pursue and eventually marry again.

Unfortunately, the cancer reoccurred and she went into complete panic and of course who amongst us would not. We began to look for the latest treatments and a more compassionate doctor than she had used in the past. We found a little of both but she was afraid to change to the doctor that I had found and continued with the one who treated her most like her father. In the end she realized what she was doing and made a change of doctor.

I worked on her while she received chemo, which helped her not to feel so sick and exhausted. The most amazing thing was that when she would come for treatment after her chemo she would drag herself in looking quite gray and frightened. By the end of the energy treatment she would actually come to life again. I would watch as the color would come into her cheeks and she would straighten her body and before long she would say "Well, I have to go. I have tickets for the theatre in New York." Amazing is all I have to say. She never left me without having been somehow injected with life from the energy.

She was so excited when she married, particularly because he wanted to marry her even through he knew her condition. He was, I must say, there until the very end. I made an exception and went to the hospital and to her home to treat her when she was trying to recover herself from infection contracted while in the hospital.

I always felt that had she not been quite so stubborn and followed just a slightly different path (I wanted her to get colonics to clean her organs but she felt if she let any chemo out of her cells she would not get full benefit of it.) she would have made it much longer and for ovarian cancer she was considered a long term survivor as it was.

I never had any illusions about a cure but certainly the energy helped her change, lose a huge amount of fear and dislike of herself and infuse her with enough life-force to survive for some many more years than would be expected. In general it definitely increased her quality of life.

Alex was another interesting case. He came to me on a whim. He had spent thirty years without being able to get any proper amount of sleep and he hated to be alone. A difficult situation when you are well over 45 years old. He was a pleasant sort of guy but definitely tough, rough, and without any belief that I could help.

We started treatments as a challenge....on his part, at least. I, of course told him about his childhood and his life and how he never felt loved by anyone in his family. He had married and divorced. His children knew that he had used drugs and had not been home for nights on end until finally his wife divorced him. For him, as with many others, it was always someone else's fault. It was never Alex who would claim any responsibility for what happened in his life and of course he picked the same kind of woman over and over and either he dropped them or they dropped him. Always for the same reason. He could never really express the loving soft side of himself.

He was always in emotional pain, concerned primarily about money. Money and material possessions were the things that made Alex feel good about himself even if it meant cheating others to make more. But although he had plenty of money and owned a lot of rented buildings, he complained about how little he had and how would he ever survive and how women only wanted his money. Why did HE always have to pay?

We worked only for a few months on and off as treatments go. He purified like crazy. He would feel angry and then depressed and then tired followed by moments of joy until finally he began to find another side of himself. Alex, after all, became soft and compassionate and caring. He now enjoyed his own company and therefore being by himself was no longer a problem.

REIKI, ENERGY, OR HOW TO FIND YOUR BLISS

So now he was enjoying life with great gusto. He was a pleasure to be with and people, including his children, could not believe that he was such a different man. Most importantly, he slept each night. Remember, this is a man who could barely get to sleep or stay asleep for over 30 years. Not bad! We had made him a believer and a very nice one, indeed.

What tale to weave for you now, dear reader, in an effort to show you how with proper evaluation, energy work and cooperation of the patient, wonders can occur. I therefore present you with Helen. Her brother who had done some intensive work with me and wanted to help his sister get off of all her medication and overcome her continuing childhood fear of being alone, referred her to me.

When she first sat down in front of me she did not know if she should scream or cry. It was not because I was frightening or ugly. Just kidding. I handed her a tissue and through her tears she told me how much medicine she was taking from so many doctors. Something for her thyroid, something for her anxiety, her depression, many pills to sleep at night and so on. She felt fat (as thin as she was) useless (although she was multi-talented) and a failure at life. I suppose it did not help much that her husband validated all of this and more as often as he could. She had little money and I agreed to work on her if she would trade one of her talents with me. It was a deal. She would do the work I needed and I would do the work she needed.

I began treatments and she began calling me at all hours of the day and night. Sometimes she would be screaming in anger, sometimes in fear and sometimes because she could not breathe or felt she was dying (panic attack). There was a time that she called and asked me to work on her while her husband took her to the emergency room. I asked that someone call me and let me know what was happening. That never came about until I called the hospital myself only to find that she had returned home.

She was a vegetarian but I felt that she was not getting any protein or enough sustenance of any kind to maintain her mind or her body. I put her with my brilliant Dr. Dulin who looked at her blood work and gave her an exact list of what to eat and what not to eat....ever. He told her what she was allergic to and why all of these things were happening. I explained that much of the underlying problem had happened when her father had died and she first began to be afraid to be alone.

Many treatments, a lot of coaching her to discipline herself with her special diet, and more discipline with her children, a suggestion of seeing a psychopharmacologist about the reaction of one medicine in relation to another and to her physiology. More time goes by and voila, we begin to slowly, over time, make a huge amount of progress. Today, we are both proud to say that she is very trim and believing it, very healthy in mind and body, and most importantly living without ANY MEDICATION. Brava Helen!

She has finished a funny little book about the Shiva-like creature that a mother must be, a website that contains her beautiful and sensitive photographs, watercolor paintings that she actively sells over an Internet site. She can go to the hairdresser without fearing that she will have to run out with color on her head because of anxiety, she enjoys her time alone at home or on drives through the country and most important to me.....no more nightly or weekly runs to the emergency room. **Energy work rules!**

In an attempt to keep you from any possibility of boredom I will give you a much deeper and more intricate insight into the depth of what can be done with a person who really wants to change and is willing to do the work without projection onto me and without refusing or eliminating any of the pieces of the puzzle that I have found necessary to deal with. The path of treatment agreed upon by both of us was kept to.

Isabella was in her twenties when she was referred to me. She was from Europe and commuted frequently between there and the United States partially for business and partially because since her father had died she felt responsible for her mother. She had always been a very family-oriented person anyway.

A physically beautiful, well-educated and talented businesswoman, she had many men who pursued her but they all terrified her. They repulsed her since her childhood. Of course everyone thought that she was just picky or had a "father issue."

As her father had been a very wealthy and prominent businessman in Europe and her mother was a timid woman who abided by most if not all of his wishes, Isabella was a mix of emotions between not wanting to be an "object" as she felt men viewed woman. She always made me laugh when she would, with her heavy accent, say the word she used for men to indicate their uselessness as she saw them. The other thing that kept me laughing was how red her slightly olive skin would become when she was angry....which was more than infrequently. Driving with her must have been quite an experience the way she told it. Yelling whenever someone was driving in her way or going too slow and God forbid it was someone in the male form. It must have been a relief that she drove expensive but rented cars.

When we began she was reticent but open to doing a series of energy treatments and in addition we spent many hours talking. This is not something I would ever do, but she was interesting and interested. Her first treatment produced a real euphoria and she always said that she wished it had been that way for the rest of our time together. She had a strong desire to change the uncomfortable, restless feelings she had experienced since childhood. She grew up in an environment in which her father and her brother were what we would call "good old boys." Most of the people in her family and the family circle of friends had the same attitude....women were to be ogled, considered definitely less than men, meant to wait on men, and definitely not smart enough to think entirely on their own....men's superior minds were needed to make "rational" decisions.

I felt that her father, although exhibiting these attitudes did indeed love her very much. He would leave a single flower on her bed and was always there to protect her and guide her. No matter, she felt extremely self-conscious when in a room full of people that included a lot of men. She told me that she hated to walk down the street wherever there were workmen because she felt they would whistle or make crude remarks about her.

We spent many an afternoon discussing every part of her life and I shared a great deal of mine with her in order to show examples of how different things were in life. We knew this was not because we were from different countries, but that we had come from families that had similar ethics, manners, cultural interest, etc. which made her feel comfortable to believe that I could help her. That she could really overcome this FEAR of men. I say fear because she was very attracted to them but also afraid.

Over time and after many treatments I invited her to join me for seminars that I had at my home to teach other of my patients a variety of things including the use of vibrational medicine based on Hanna Kroeger's herbs and healing waters, the effect of scent oils, the healing methods of Peruvian shamans, mantra chanting lessons with my friend Turkantam who came from France to tour with his CDs and teach. He had been the musician for Mahavatar, Babaji in India, who is my teacher and his.

My friend Nina Murphy who taught many of these classes, spent time with Isabella and over time we put together some of the old pieces that made sense now. You may not be one to believe in anything but the present life, but we do and did and this gave so much explanation to Isabella's fears both of men and having children.

In this life, Isabella's family, although European, had an unusual relationship with the American indigenous people. Her father and brother both hunted both locally and throughout Europe and many times her father would like to watch American movies of the indigenous people and mimic in certain ways, some of their culture. He taught Isabella all about nature including the names, sounds and habits of birds and other animals. He seemed to have a deep understanding of these people and the times that they lived in.

What became interesting to me was not how much Isabella related to them but how much she disliked anything from the American West or certain places in the Northeast woods. The pioneers who traveled by covered wagon were most repugnant to her. She was knowledgeable about guns and hunting from her father and was fascinated. She had been taught how to load, clean and aim hunting guns. I am not saying that this is uncommon, but to have such an interest and dislike of things that she had never experienced in her own country was not so simple a thought to me.

So when, during her many different regressions she experienced many horrible things happening to her I did not find it unusual. She saw herself being beaten by men, her children being killed and once she saw her belly opened and her unborn child killed. Now a lot of her feelings began to make sense to her and to me. It gave her more of an acceptance about her life and a possible explanation for her fears.

Nina Murphy explained to her that she felt much too much responsibility for both her mother and the family in general. Isabella used to travel to her family in Europe over a long weekend, many times returning immediately after to finish her work in this country.

She went to a party at a friend's house in New York and called me the next day to say that her friend had given her phone number to a man at the party that was very attracted to her. I was sure that she would be furious, but no. Many people that she met through business wanted her to meet their brother or a friend and always she politely refused. This time, she called and said that the gentleman had called her and she was going to the symphony with him. Was I shocked? You bet!

This developed into a relationship of some merit. It took a lot of treatments and a lot of talks, but after three months she let him hold her hand. Ok, she was still traveling overseas to the family just as often (much to his dislike) but she did see him often for dinner or concerts and so on whenever she was in this country.

Finally she called and announced that she had gone to bed with him and had sex for the first time in her life. I considered this something to celebrate and we did. What wonderment. She was not thrilled with it but with the fact that she had overcome her longtime fear and had taken the biggest risk of her life. Now, who knew what she would do. He eventually wanted to marry her. He gave her beautiful gifts and professed his love for her. It was too bad for him, because she did not join him in those thoughts.

She learned to meditate, to do Reiki for herself, to follow her intuitive ability and to use a lot of it in the business world. She continued not to understand why women stayed in relationships that were unhappy for them, but after a huge love affair with a man so unacceptable to her and her lifestyle she began to learn what it was to have exceptional sex because it was combined with intense love. Isabella softened about so many things. She became much more understanding of both men and women and why they behaved as they did. She learned well AND applied what I taught her about the perceived Unavailable Parent until she could see the clues as fast as I could.

Time passed and she grew in leaps and bounds. Even on the occasions when I talk to her today I am amazed at the courage she had and the journey that she continues to travel.

I consider Isabella to be, most probably, one of two of the best results of my work. In this case it took a lot of time and work. I am sorry that she does not live in this country and that she travels here infrequently. I would now enjoy her as a real friend.

This brings me to the secret of how to find YOUR bliss. I have spoken all along of what to do but here it is again.

FIND YOUR PATTERN...DO ENERGY WORK TO REMOVE THE BLOCKS...SURRENDER TO WHATEVER YOU CONSIDER THE DIVINE.

IF YOU REMEMBER ANYTHING REMEMBER THE WORDS OF MY TEACHER, BABAJI AND BEGIN TO LIVE.

TRUTH   SIMPLICITY   LOVE

*"Two things are infinite: the universe
and human stupidity, and I'm not sure
about the universe"*

ALBERT EINSTEIN

"Intellectuals solve problems. Geniuses prevent them."

ALBERT EINSTEIN

"Human beings pine for love in this
world without which life is empty.
When love is intense, unconditional,
and devoid of expectations, it
transforms into divine love. True
fulfillment and unbounded joy can
come only from divine love."
UNKNOWN

Behold this dreamer cometh

GENESIS 37:19

In addition to the usual sources, this book can be
ordered from: www.maxinegaudio.com

or submit the following order form & payment to:
HAJI and BABU press llc
P. O. Box 196
Old Greenwich, CT 06870

BOOK ORDER FORM
(Int'l. orders, and book sellers, please write to above.)

NAME: _____

ADDRESS: _____

_____

CITY: _____

STATE: _____

ZIP CODE: _____

METHODS OF PAYMENT ACCEPTED:
Check, U.S. Postal Service money order, or the following:

Visa ☐   Mastercard ☐   American Express ☐

CARD NUMBER: _____

CARD EXPIRATION DATE (MM/YY): _____

NAME ON CARD: _____

SECURITY CODE*: _____

*This is the last 3 numbers on back of Visa or Mastercard, or the small
4 numbers on the front of American Express card.*

BOOK PRICE: $42.95 (US) + $4.60 Priority Mail = $47.55
(Shipments to Connecticut must add 6% sales tax.)
*An order for multiple books to be shipped to the same address will be
packaged together to reduce mailing costs.*

Printed in the United States
133425LV00003B/129/P